Bringing the Human Being Back to Work

Tim Baker

Bringing the Human Being Back to Work

The 10 Performance and Development Conversations Leaders Must Have

Tim Baker
WINNERS-at-WORK Pty Ltd.
Brisbane, QLD, Australia

ISBN 978-3-319-93171-5 (hardcover)   ISBN 978-3-319-93172-2 (eBook)
ISBN 978-3-030-06606-2 (softcover)
https://doi.org/10.1007/978-3-319-93172-2

Library of Congress Control Number: 2018946148

© The Editor(s) (if applicable) and The Author(s) 2019, First softcover printing 2021
This work is subject to copyright. All rights are solely and exclusively licensed by the Publisher, whether the whole or part of the material is concerned, specifically the rights of translation, reprinting, reuse of illustrations, recitation, broadcasting, reproduction on microfilms or in any other physical way, and transmission or information storage and retrieval, electronic adaptation, computer software, or by similar or dissimilar methodology now known or hereafter developed.
The use of general descriptive names, registered names, trademarks, service marks, etc. in this publication does not imply, even in the absence of a specific statement, that such names are exempt from the relevant protective laws and regulations and therefore free for general use.
The publisher, the authors and the editors are safe to assume that the advice and information in this book are believed to be true and accurate at the date of publication. Neither the publisher nor the authors or the editors give a warranty, express or implied, with respect to the material contained herein or for any errors or omissions that may have been made. The publisher remains neutral with regard to jurisdictional claims in published maps and institutional affiliations.

Cover credit: IR_Stone / iStock / Getty Images Plus
Cover design by Tom Howey

Printed on acid-free paper

This Palgrave Macmillan imprint is published by the registered company Springer International Publishing AG part of Springer Nature.
The registered company address is: Gewerbestrasse 11, 6330 Cham, Switzerland

To Glen Crowther, an outstanding English teacher, who loved his work, challenged his students to better things ("The Pursuit of Excellence"), inspired me to be a writer.

Preface

The enterprise of humankind is what's missing in work settings across the globe. People have become robots at work, and from what we're being told, robots will soon replace people. How ironic!

An organization—any organization—is a bunch of people working together toward a common goal. We tend to lose sight of this simple idea. Managers are preoccupied with processes, procedures, methods, and systems. For the past 100 years, we've progressively dehumanized our places of work—although many argue that the workplace was never humanized! We've learnt to systemize, homogenize, and mechanize human work—all in the quest for greater efficiency and cost-saving. We've forgotten that the human being is the epicenter of work.

We performance manage people at work. They receive a job specification and job description, submit to a performance appraisal once or twice a year—all in the name of *performance management*. In between these management rituals, the employee is expected to follow instructions, not upset the apple cart, and stick to the straight and narrow. Despite the rhetoric to the contrary, people are viewed as a resource—a small cog in the large wheel of production.

We label people at work as *human capital*, or worse: a *human resource*. These labels dehumanize people and turn them into an abstract piece of the machinery of production. Human resources are lumped in with technological resources, administrative resources, and financial resources. Human beings are expected to leave their humanness at the door of the business and become a compliant business resource to be manipulated to accomplish predetermined business outcomes.

The business world is indeed a cold, clinical, rational domain, devoid of humanness. Human resources—which has become an industry in its own right—has complicated things in its attempt to legitimize its existence. We've downsized, upsized, and rightsized the workforce. We've up-skilling, down-skilled, and multi-skilling our human resources. We've got function-based work, project-based work, key performance indicators, and key result areas. And it goes on. Where does the human being fit within the debased professional jargon of HR?

We sense this dehumanization process. We make fun of it. It leads to Dilbert-like jokes and parodies such as *The Office* on TV. We've lost sight of the fundamentals of humanness. Organizations strive to be high performing, maneuverable, and agile. But to achieve these attributes, leaders need to get the best from the people who work for them. Enterprises need—more than ever—a competitive or adaptive advantage in a hyper-aggressive and warp speed marketplace. The cliché we keep hearing and using nauseatingly is that *people are our competitive advantage*. Paradoxically, we make our places of work less—not more—human.

My mission in *Bringing the Human Being Back to Work: The 10 Performance and Development Conversations Leaders Must Have* is to bring the human being back to work. How can we put people front and center of organizational life? How can we get employees to act as the people they are away from the workplace—at home? What do leaders need to do to make this happen? Why isn't it happening now? What are the roadblocks? These are the big questions I want to explore with you in the pages ahead.

The answer isn't necessary about being kind, gentle, and caring. Although I'm sure you'd agree—more of that wouldn't go astray! There's a pragmatic edge to my book. I want people to give more of themselves at work. You do too. The aim is to get the best from people—to ignite their human spirit in the organizational work they do. The enterprise of humankind is what's missing in work settings across the globe. People have become robots at work, and from what we're being told, robots will soon replace people. How ironic!

Conversation holds the key. I'm convinced they are our salvation. Conversations are powerful and underestimated. They are the tool to humanize work. Would you agree: We aren't having enough authentic conversations at work? And I'm not necessarily referring to the 'tough' conversations. I'm referring to *any* developmental or performance conversations. Far easier to press a button and send a text or email. We rationalize that it's faster, and simpler—easier. It saves time. And 'time is money,' as we're frequently told.

We've lost sight of what matters and makes a difference—the human element of work. I'm not promoting the idea of people sit around all day at work having idle chit-chat. I'm not interested in that kind of conversation—social conversations occur anyhow. Developmental and performance conversations, when done well, can bring the best out in people. These conversations guide, inform, influence, encourage, and clarify. Conversation is two-way—it's essentially about treating people as partners, as equals. It's the human thing to do.

Most people I speak with think that the idea of bringing the human being back to work is a wonderful idea. But how and what do we discuss? Where do we start? The *how* is through developmental and performance conversations—one conversation at a time. The *what* is the type of conversations we purposely choose to have. The *where* is anywhere, at any time. *The 10 Performance and Development Conversations Leaders Must Have* categorizes the most important conversations into a series of themes—10—as the title states. I'm providing you with a roadmap for people-centered conversations.

Some people say to me: *We aren't ready yet to have conversations?* Really? I feel like responding by asking these managers: *When do you think you'll be ready?* The fastest and best way to create a culture of conversation is to start having more people-centered conversations.

When will you be *ready*? You may never be *ready*. So, the best thing to do is start practicing now. With practice, the quality of conversation improves. If every leader in your organization buys into this idea, you'll have a conversation culture in no time. With regularity and an emphasis on performance and development, trust builds and work engagement increases. Human spirit and work integrate to become a powerful, productive force.

What are these 10 conversations about?

You need frameworks, models, blueprints, and tools to get started. You'll get this from the book. It's not as simple as inviting leaders to devote more time to conversing with their team members—it needs more than just creating time and space. It won't happen automatically—despite most leaders thinking it's a terrific idea to do so. Busyness gets in the way. The excuses start: *I'm too busy to have conversations; I haven't got time to have conversations; I have work to do; Once I get all this work done, I'll have time for conversations.* These common alibis are based on the erroneous assumption that conversations aren't productive and take up too much time. People-centered conversations are considered *nice* to have, not necessary *must* haves.

So, to make developmental and performance conversations a priority, you need a game plan. This book offers you the plan. I articulate the benefits of these conversations—reduced turnover, heightened engagement, trust building, increased productivity and performance, alignment of perspectives, enhanced influence, and many other advantages. I also explore some of the reasons meaningful workplace conversations are disintegrating and how this erosion can be arrested. We consider 10 significant conversations leaders can have to humanize their place of work.

More specifically, *The 10 Performance and Development Conversations Leaders Must Have* is broken into three parts. Part I is about cultivating an authentic workplace based on people-centered conversations. Why conversations? Why are they so effective and yet so neglected? What's the pay-off for authentic conversations? What's the essence of being authentic? We get to these questions straight away.

Part II covers developmental conversations leaders should engage with team members frequently. I cover five types of conversations: the coaching conversation, the delegation conversation, the visioning conversation, the encouraging conversation, and the relationship building conversation. Many conversations are a mix of these themes. Nonetheless, by using these five themes, it reminds us to make sure we're having these kinds of conversations regularly.

Part III envelops five performance conversations leaders ought to be having too. This collection of conversations I call the *Five Conversations Framework*. This framework can be a substitute for the traditional performance review. Many organizations around the world—large, medium and small, public, private and not-for-profit—have adopted this framework with wonderful results. Whether the framework replaces the standard performance review or not, it provides a great structure for five more salient but overlooked performance conversations.

I hope you enjoy my book and it helps you to either build a new culture of conversation or improve your capacity to lead human beings at work. I can promise you this: If you prioritize these conversations, you'll be a spark plug for enhanced morale, increased job satisfaction, better team work, and ultimately, improved personal and organizational productivity within your sphere of influence. And you'll enjoy yourself too!

I wish you well on your evolving leadership journey.

Brisbane, QLD, Australia   Tim Baker

Contents

Part I	**Cultivating an Authentic Workplace**	1
1	**The Dumbing Down of Work**	3
	The Birth of Specialization	5
	The Dehumanization of Work	7
	The Top 10 Key Points ...	10
2	**Human Spirit and Work**	13
	What Is Human Spirit and Work?	13
	Autonomy	16
	Mastery	16
	Purpose	17
	The Top 10 Key Points ...	18
3	**The Concept of Workplace Dignity**	21
	Workplace Dignity	23
	The Top 10 Key Points ...	28
4	**A Lack of Authentic Conversations**	31
	Authentic Conversations	34
	The Top 10 Key Points ...	37
5	**Two Task-focused Pillars of Authentic Conversations**	39
	Pillar 1: Agree on Expectations	42
	Pillar 2: Challenge Unhelpful Behavior	44
	The Top 10 Key Points ...	46

Contents

6	**Three People-focused Pillars of Authentic Conversations**	49
	Pillar 3: Establish a Trusting Relationship	49
	Pillar 4: Show Genuine Appreciation	52
	Pillar 5: Build for the Future	55
	The Top 10 Key Points …	58

Part II Five Developmental Conversations 61

7	**Conversation 1: The Coaching Conversation**	63
	Corridor Coaching	67
	The Top 10 Key Points …	69
8	**Using GROW for a Better Coaching Conversation**	71
	Goal	71
	Reality	72
	Options	73
	What Next?	74
	The Rationale for Using GROW	75
	The Top 10 Key Points …	77
9	**Conversation 2: The Delegation Conversation**	79
	Why Don't Managers Delegate?	80
	The Top 10 Key Points …	84
10	**Ten Keys to a Better Delegation Conversation**	87
	1. Freedom and Autonomy	87
	2. Delegation of Authority	88
	3. Kept Informed	89
	4. Don't Interfere	89
	5. Don't Countermand	89
	6. Delegating too Infrequently	90
	7. The Buck Stops with Me	91
	8. Experience and Abilities	91
	9. Don't Delegate only Routine Work	92
	10. Breathing Down Their Neck	92
	The Top 10 Key Points …	93
11	**Conversation 3: The Visioning Conversation**	95
	The Top 10 Key Points …	99

12	**Visioning Tools for Group and Individual Conversations**	101
	Six Visioning Questions	101
	Team Values Charter	102
	The Top 10 Key Points …	105
13	**Conversation 4: The Encouraging Conversation**	107
	Thank-you	109
	Encouragement and Engagement	110
	The Top 10 Key Points …	111
14	**Twelve Powerful Ways to Engage or Disengage People at Work**	113
	Expectations	113
	Materials and Equipment	114
	Opportunity	114
	Recognition	114
	Caring	115
	Development	115
	Opinions	116
	Relevance	116
	Commitment	117
	Friendship	118
	Progress	118
	Learning and Growing	119
	The Top 10 Key Points …	120
15	**Conversation 5: The Relationship Building Conversation**	123
	Relationships and Tasks	125
	Trust	125
	Openness, Appreciation, and Interest	128
	Empathetic Listening	129
	The Top 10 Key Points …	130
16	**Five Steps to Relationship Building Conversations**	133
	Step 1: Show Up	134
	Step 2: Listen Up	134
	Step 3: Speak Up	135
	Step 4: Lift Up	136
	Step 5: Follow Up	137
	The Top 10 Key Points …	138

Contents

Part III   Five Performance Conversations — 141

17   Overview of the Five Conversations Framework — 143
  Benefits of the Five Conversations Framework — 147
  The Top 10 Key Points … — 148

18   Rationale and Benefits of the Five Conversations Framework — 151
  Climate Review Conversation — 152
  Strengths and Talents Conversation — 153
  Opportunities for Growth Conversation — 153
  Learning and Development Conversation — 154
  Innovation and Continuous Improvement Conversation — 154
  Ongoing Dialogue — 156
  Open and Direct — 157
  Flexible — 157
  Timely Information — 157
  Relaxed — 158
  The Top 10 Key Points … — 158

19   Conversation 6: The Climate Review Conversation — 161
  What's a Climate Review? — 162
  Value Alignment — 163
  Benchmarking Tool — 164
  More Clarity — 165
  Taking and Reviewing Action — 165
  What Questions to Ask? — 165
  The Top 10 Key Points … — 169

20   Conversation 7: The Strengths and Talents Conversation — 171
  Our Obsession with Strengthening Weaknesses — 172
  The Rule of the Three Ps — 175
  What Questions to Ask? — 175
  Strategies for Reshaping Roles — 176
    Job Rotation — 177
    Job Enrichment — 177
    Job Enlargement — 177
    Multi-skilling — 178
  The Top 10 Key Points … — 179

21	**Conversation 8: The Opportunities for Growth Conversation**	181
	Awareness	183
	Timing	183
	Frame-of-mind	184
	The Ideal Outcome of the Conversation	184
	Allow Them to Reflect on Their Performance	185
	Offer Feedback	185
	Be Objective	186
	Use a Problem-solving Approach	186
	Think About All Factors	187
	Ask Questions and Listen	187
	What Questions to Ask?	188
	The Top 10 Key Points …	190
22	**Conversation 9: The Learning and Development Conversation**	193
	What is Learning and Development?	194
	Technical-centered	195
	Person-centered	196
	Problem-centered	196
	Multidimensional Approach to Learning	197
	What Questions to Ask?	198
	The Top 10 Key Points …	200
23	**Conversation 10: The Innovation and Continuous Improvement Conversation**	203
	A Mindset of Stability and Predictability	204
	The Difference Between Innovation and Continuous Improvement	207
	What Questions to Ask?	208
	Assessing Ideas	211
	Time	211
	Complexity	211
	Cost	212
	The Top 10 Key Points …	213

Index   215

Part I

Cultivating an Authentic Workplace

1

The Dumbing Down of Work

Work can offer more than a source of income; it ought to be a vehicle for personal growth, wellbeing, providing a sense of belonging, and fulfilling purpose and direction in one's life.

Stanford University researcher, Mark Lepper and his team conducted a significant research study in the early 1970s, concerned with the impact of extrinsic rewards on performance. Specifically, Lepper was interested in whether prizes influence behavior in young children.

A brand-new activity was introduced to the children at a nursery. The teachers issued the children with creamy white artist's drawing paper and brand-new marker pens; the children were given time to draw with these novel materials. They had never done drawings with marker pens before. Predictably, the children took to the activity with relish. But after exactly one hour, the materials were whisked away to the disappointment of the children.

Several days later, one of the researchers returned to the class and randomly divided the class into two groups to continue the new drawing activity. One group of children were taken to another room. They were given the opportunity to continue their drawings, just as they had done before. After an hour, the researcher thanked the children in this group and took away the art material and their drawings.

The second group of children were offered a prize for drawing their pictures. It was explained to this group that some special prizes would be given to the children who draw good pictures. The children took to their task, anticipating they might receive a prize for their picture. This control group was given the same amount of time (one hour) as the other group to compete their art work. At the end of the session, the researcher thanked the children as he'd done with the other group. But this time, he handed out a prize to each child in the control group.

One week later the researchers returned to the classroom. The afternoon period consisted of 'free time;' the children could choose what they wanted to do with their time. The special paper and marker pens were placed on the tables and easily accessible to the children. However, the children had other options too. They could go outside and run around in the playground. They could play with the toys in the classroom. Or they could return to the drawing activity. The researchers observed the time the children spent on their chosen activities. To what extent would the prizes given to the children in the control group affect their choices and behavior? The researchers assumed that the children in the control group, who had received prizes, would spend more time on the drawing activity.

But that didn't happen!

The result was one the researchers didn't foresee. Their findings challenged conventional wisdom about parenting and education. The children who received the extrinsic rewards for their art work chose to spend less time drawing than those who weren't rewarded. Conversely, the children who didn't receive a prize chose to spend more of their discretionary time on the drawing activity. The children who were rewarded seemed reluctant to continue with the activity without the promise of a further reward. The initial reward paradoxically reduced the children's motivation rather than increase it.

But what was even more surprising is this: The art work of all the children was evaluated by a group of independent judges with no knowledge of the experiment. The result was that the pictures drawn by the children who were rewarded were evaluated as less competent than the pictures drawn by the unrewarded group.

So, in summary, the children who received an extrinsic reward spent less time drawing when given a choice, and when they were rewarded, they put in less effort too.[1]

The birth of 'scientific management' was the beginning of the systemic dehumanization of the workplace. Frederick Taylor was widely regarded as the architect of scientific management. Taylor introduced his method in the early part of the last century in factories, such as the *Ford Motor Company*. His mission was to improve business economy, and scientific management proved a success in systemizing efficiency. The early twentieth century workplace was transformed into a sequence of processes, systems, and procedures. Systems replaced people. Freedom of expression of how people carried out their job was taken away for the first time in industrial history. People's individual choices, preferences, and approaches to getting their job done were subordinated to 'time and motion' studies. These findings determined the 'one best way' of doing all manual work in the factory.

With Taylor's systemization of work and the division of responsibility between the role of manager and employee, the start of specialization took hold of the factory floor.

The Birth of Specialization

Scientific management redesigned the work environment; it alienated workers from management. One of its core principles was, and sadly still is to a large extent, that management does the *thinking* and workers do the *work*. Specialization also estranged the worker from the work itself. Breaking work down into small, monotonous, and simple component parts—although undoubtedly easier to control—was the genesis for job specification. It made work predictable, dull, and repetitive. After an early success, high absenteeism, and other negative consequences, started to gain a foothold. Job specialization is still a feature 100 years later. But specialization challenges the modern concept of agility. Agility and adaptability are more relevant now than precision and specialization.

Marketing products and services across different locations and cultures requires responsiveness and nimbleness, for example. Being adaptable and malleable can't readily be documented in a generic job specification.

Specialization is pervasive in the world of work. Systemic specialization began on the assembly line. Each worker was expected to perform a few simple tasks in a recurring fashion. Job specialization eventually found its way into service industries too. The big success story in the service sector, for instance, is the *McDonalds Corporation*. The McDonald's franchise operation is modern scientific management personified. McDonalds was the first fast-food restaurant chain to successfully apply divisions of specialization; one person takes the orders, while someone else makes the burgers, another person applies the condiments, and yet another wraps them. With this level of efficiency, the customer generally receives a product and service with reliable quality.

So how is the universal specialization of work dehumanizing?

Predicable and repetitive work practices inevitably dull the human spirit. Engaging people in this kind of work is challenging. Inducements were introduced to engage employees. But it's contestable whether extrinsic rewards work, as the research at the beginning of the chapter suggests.

The person who wants to be creative and innovative is likely to be frustrated and disappointed with this approach. When confronted with an endless procession of standardized processes and procedures to follow, the enterprising employee will most probably disengage. Questioning the status quo isn't valued to the same extent as following the status quo. Questioning the status quo can be career diminishing, not career enhancing.

Further, specialization implies that the specialist *knows best*. Specialists stick to established practices. Proposing a new method in a procedure-driven environment infers the *old* system is somehow inferior or substandard. The current system may need a makeover. But standard practice is often vigorously defended. The proposed new method is therefore rejected outright.

Work specialization breeds tunnel vision. The specialist employee cannot—and doesn't necessarily want to—understand or appreciate the way the rest of the organization operates. With blinkers on, the employee concentrates all their energies on the few, manageable work tasks written in their job description. Grasping the interdependencies of the moving parts that make up the organizational structure is like looking simultaneously at the road ahead and the surroundings while driving.

Apart from job fixation, enthusiasm for a constrained bandwidth of tasks can wane too. This is another challenge for managing work quality. Specialization can cultivate resistance, or at the very least disengagement. Friction centers on management's quest to closely measure effort and productivity—what we know commonly referred to as *micromanagement*. The job-holder's agency and autonomy ultimately surrender to management control and restriction. Excessive regulation and the resultant forfeiting of individual liberty unsurprisingly lead to shrinking levels of motivation.

Although there's valid justification and evidence of success, applying the *one best way*—repetitiously doing rudimentary tasks—dehumanizes work. People's spirit and the work they do are separated like a fork in the road.

As a tradeoff for simplifying work, management uses incentives to keep the job-holder content. These inducements are designed to preserve and boost performance on the job. At their best, extrinsic rewards merely satisfy employees, however. They do little else. And a satisfied employee is not necessarily a productive one.

There is a myth that job performance and job satisfaction go together like strawberries and cream. There's no conclusive evidence to definitively prove job performance and job satisfaction are linked.[2] This misguided belief has led to a performance management regime based on incentives intended to satisfy people at work.

But *carrots* don't necessarily boost sustainable performance. Cultivating the conditions for intrinsic motivation to take hold is a more potent way of amplifying performance. Engaging 'hearts and minds' is poles apart from arousing job satisfaction with extrinsic rewards. Shifting from extrinsic to intrinsic motivational methods means rethinking performance management.

People still need to be paid properly and given rewards and incentives for top performance, of course. But alluring human spirit at work is a different matter.

Work itself holds the key to unlocking personal commitment and productivity. Rather than chopping organizational work into small, dull, repetitive, and unchallenging component parts, another way of deploying people begs serious consideration. The peripheral recompenses for completing prescribed work tasks is only one piece of a large jigsaw. We need more pieces to finish the picture.

Is it too idealistic to think that human spirit and work can coexist in the workplace? Is it unrealistic to assume that people can be aroused by the work they do, rather than be comfortable with the rewards they receive? I don't think so.

But we first must question the deeply rooted belief that pay and conditions bring the best out in people. Peripheral incentives are akin to the starting gate position in a horse race. It's important but not everything. The reward and punishment technique—born from the psychological concept of operant conditioning[3]—is still the guiding principle of performance management. What's more, it's not the cure-all we've been led to believe. This is particularly the case when it comes to our increasingly educated workforce. I'd like to suggest that one of the hallmarks of an authentic workplace is evidence of the engagement of human spirit.

The Dehumanization of Work

The 'humanist movement' was largely a response to the philosophy and principles of scientific management. The main criticism of scientific management by *humanists*[4] is the dehumanization of workers. Scientific management was originally intended to stop workers thinking about their work. By separating the planning and execution of work, workers needn't bother to think—thinking being the domain of management. As I wrote in *Performance Management for Agile Organizations,*

This division of *planning* and *doing*—as logical as it indubitably seems—strips the worker of their autonomy and self-sufficiency. Mastery of work in these circumstances boiled down to robotically and repetitiously following a series of processes or procedures.[5]

Work broken down into simple, controllable segments will inevitably lack any real meaning for the job-holder. Unsurprisingly, humanists railed against this dumbing down of work.

Dave and Wendy Ulrich in their book *The Why of Work: How Great Leaders Build Abundant Organizations That Win* explain the significance of understanding how work contributes to a greater cause beyond simply completing a set of work tasks.[6] I acknowledged earlier that work has transformed prodigiously since the days of the factory assembly line. But the way we still design work and manage performance hasn't evolved at anywhere near the same pace. We still unquestioningly persist with many of the outdated principles of scientific management. Work is still segmented, regimented, and tightly controlled.

Dan Pink in his popular book, *Drive: The Surprising Truth about Motivation*, challenges us to think completely differently about human motivation and performance.[7] He reinforces my view that the carrot and stick approach isn't always the best way of creating a motivational work environment. This is especially relevant for the educated twenty-first-century knowledge worker. Pink suggests we need to do more than placate job-holders with a sprinkling of tangible incentives.

Where the Rubber Meets the Road…

Lessons from the Circus

Like many parents, I enjoy taking my children to the circus and seeing the wonderment in their eyes from the spectacle. Year after year, I take our youngest daughter to the circus for that reason. It's a great joy for us both. The colors, sounds, and smells; it's all an intoxicating sensory delight.

My daughter mostly likes the show ponies. The trainer has a light whip in one hand and a pocket full of treats in the other. During the show, the trainer uses both the whip and treats to coax the ponies to do their impressive feats.

It makes me think: This isn't far removed from the way we try to motivate human beings in the workplace. In fact, it's the same! Human beings are treated like circus animals in the main. The manager dangles carrots in front of employees in the form of extrinsic rewards, such as bonuses, and use sanctions to punish when someone step out of line.

In the circus tent, reward and punishment seems to work splendidly to get the animals to perform. But does it work as well in the educated workplace of the twenty-first century?

After all, rewards and punishment is simple to understand, easy to monitor, and straightforward to administer.[8]

There's nothing wrong with being satisfied with work. There are many benefits with work satisfaction. A satisfied employee is more energized compared with an unsatisfied employee, for instance. A satisfied employee is less inclined to run off and work for a competitor than an unsatisfied employee. It's generally good to be satisfied with the work one does.

But it's a mistake to think that job satisfaction automatically translates to good performance.

Work performance is complex—it involves lots of moving parts. Performance is a combination of factors within and beyond the job-holder. How the person sees oneself has a bearing on work performance, for instance. A host of factors come into play when the job-holder interacts with the work environment too. And another set of factors are associated with the job of work itself. It's complicated.

The idea of placating workers originated from scientific management. Paradoxically, Taylor designed work in part to satisfy workers. Rewards and incentives were introduced to encourage people to do what they were told. Being told what to do, how to do it, and how long to take, robs the worker of their agency and initiative. So, on the surface, it's hard to understand how overly systemized work could be in the interests of pleasing workers. Taylor explains the connection between scientific management and job satisfaction:

> The task is always so regulated that the man who is well suited to his job will thrive while working at this rate during a long term of years and grow happier and more prosperous, instead of being overworked.[9]

Taylor believed in the value of monetary incentives. According to Taylor, work "consists mainly of simple, not particularly interesting, tasks. The only way to get people to do them is to incentivize them properly and monitor them carefully."[10] This kind of thinking is still prevalent today. The significant disparity, however, is that education standards are much higher, and the nature of work is unrecognizable from the factory assembly line. Not only has work transformed, the work we now do has the potential to be more stimulating and self-directed, notwithstanding the way it is organized.

We should therefore consider how work can ignite the human spirit. How can we organize work to be more meaningful and engaging? What is the leader's role? Apart from relying upon tangible rewards to satisfy employees, there's plenty of untapped scope to engage the human spirit in work. We'll peruse these ideas in the next chapter.

The Top 10 Key Points …

1. The introduction of scientific management dehumanized the workplace.
2. With Frederick Taylor's systemization of work and the division of responsibility between the roles of management and employee, the birth of specialization took hold of the factory assembly line.
3. Predicable and repetitive work practices inevitably dull the human spirit.
4. One of scientific management's core principles was that management would do the thinking and workers would do the work.
5. Being adaptable and malleable can't readily be documented in a generic job specification.
6. To compensate for the dumbing down of work, managers implement a suite of extrinsic rewards around employment incentives and conditions to satisfy the job-holder and attempt to increase performance.
7. It's a mistake to think that job satisfaction automatically results in good performance.
8. Cultivating the conditions for intrinsic motivation to take hold, is a more effective way of enhancing performance.
9. Work performance is complex; it involves lots of moving parts.
10. Incentivizing employees with monetary rewards is still considered the pathway to good performance.

Notes

1. Yeung, R. (2011). I is for influence: The new science of persuasion. London: Macmillan.
2. Judge, T.A., Bono, J.E., Thoresen, C.J., & Patton, G.K. (2001). The job satisfaction-job performance relationship: A qualitative and quantitative review. *Psychological Bulletin*, 127, 3, 376–407.
3. *Operant conditioning* is a type of learning where behavior is controlled by consequences. Key concepts in operant conditioning are positive reinforcement, negative reinforcement, positive punishment and negative punishment.
4. *Humanism* is a philosophical and ethical stance that emphasizes the value and agency of human beings, individually and collectively.
5. Baker, T.B. (2016). Performance management for agile organizations: Overthrowing the eight management myths that hold businesses back. London: Palgrave Macmillan.

6. Ulrich, D. & Ulrich, W. (2010). The why of work: How great leaders build abundant organizations that win. USA: McGraw-Hill.
7. Pink, D.H. (2009). Drive: The surprising truth about what motivates us. USA: Riverhead Books.
8. Baker, T.B. (2016). Performance management for agile organizations: Overthrowing the eight management myths that hold businesses back. London: Palgrave Macmillan.
9. Taylor, F.A. (1919). The principles of scientific management. New York: Harper & Brothers.
10. Pink, D.H. (2009). Drive: The surprising truth about what motivates us. USA: Riverhead Books.

2

Human Spirit and Work

Believing in the work we do is the stepping stone to higher achievement.

In the first chapter, we considered some of the roadblocks to engage employees, born out of the scientific management movement of the early twentieth century. We've persevered with the carrot and stick to motivate employees to give their best within the narrow corridor of the job specification. If we consider the plethora of engagement survey results worldwide, this approach has largely failed. We need a new method to structuring work. In this chapter, we look at the concept of *human spirit and work* and some of the available avenues for igniting personal motivation.

What Is Human Spirit and Work?

The mission to find meaning in work—what Abraham Maslow called *self-actualization*—isn't new. In concert with the Hawthorne studies[1] in the 1930s, the human relation movement was interested in employee happiness at work. This movement, as I indicated, responded to the hard edge of the scientific management that took root a few decades earlier. Now, a century later, with the mindboggling transformations in the world and the rise of the knowledge worker, there's a rekindling of enthusiasm for finding deeper purpose in work, beyond paying off the mortgage.

But the concept of human spirit and work sounds like an oxymoron! Let me define it.

By human spirit, I'm not referring to religion conversion, or getting people to buy into some sort of belief system. What it means is people—partially or fully—having their spiritual needs nourished through the work they do. The concept of human spirit and work is about discovering one's identity and sense of purpose through work. Further, it's about gaining a feeling of self-worth from work—not losing it. This feeling of self-esteem goes well beyond feeling satisfied with having a job. Human spirit and work is the immersion of one's human spirit in their work role. Awakening and feeding a person's spirit at work have benefits for the individual, the organization, and society-at-large.

Most people want more from work than only a job. But job-holders are usually told what to do, how to do it, and when to do it. Unconventional thinking and behavior on-the-job is at best frowned upon, despite the rampant rhetoric of the need to be agile and innovative. People are put into strait jackets and expected to fly.

As we've discussed, extrinsic rewards have limitations in promoting the human spirit at work. They can even demotivate. People generally want more than the promise of a bonus from their work. Work can proffer other gains besides an income. Personal growth, wellbeing, a sense of belonging, and purpose and direction in one's life are some such benefits. These potential non-monetary bonuses of work can't be met with just a pay check.

Sometimes these work incentives can be counterproductive.

When an incentive is used to increase performance, it can do the opposite. An incentive can unintendedly take the employee's eye off the task the reward is designed to improve. The allure of an inducement shifts the focus from the task to the prize. The work becomes the means to reaching the outcome—a reward. As the research in the last chapter illustrates, extrinsic rewards can diminish—not increase—performance. With a bonus top-of-mind, it's common for the employee to cut corners, do whatever it takes, or even cheat, to get their hands on the *prize*. It's like an athlete taking banned substances to win a gold medal at the Olympics. As well intended as extrinsic rewards are—and as effective as they can sometimes be—they can promote unintended and unwelcome behavior.

Nonetheless, inducing greater performance using monetary incentives has been part of the DNA of the work-setting since the dawn of industry. Workers were once viewed—and perhaps still are in many ways—as small cogs in a large factory machine. Bonus pay is still used to entice workers to conform and perform. Cogs in a machine perform a limited range of activity. And so too it is with job design. While oil and adjustments are used to keep cogs working, carrot and stick are the levers to fortify obedience and productivity in humans. This has been the way for over 100 years. Just like training show ponies, we've persevered with a suite of inducements and sanctions to cajole performance. As work is transforming before our very eyes, the way we kindle human productivity hasn't kept pace.

The underlying assumption is that the best way to get human beings to behave correctly is to use the 'pain/pleasure principle,' that is, reward desirable behavior and punish undesirable behavior. It can work. But it's one-dimensional.

I'm arguing that we need to consider other more intrinsic motivational forces.

If the primary purpose of doing a job of work is to receive a pay packet and the odd bonus, organizational work won't elevate a person's wellbeing past *paying the bills*. Though many employees are undoubtedly satisfied with this arrangement, it's hardly a recipe for inspired work performance.

So, what's the solution? How is human spirit captivated in the workplace? Are there other ways beside the carrot and stick to boost performance?

Dan Pink makes the case that the intrinsic motivational pathway is a more attractive option to the contemporary, self-lead knowledge worker. Pink asserts that it's time to move past the carrot and stick as a tool of motivation. Authentic motivation comes from within. Believing in the work we do and its purpose is the stepping stone to higher achievement. Instead of using the dual levers of rewards and punishment to control human work production, we ought to take a closer look at the work itself. What people do (and don't do) at work and how it's structured is often overlooked as the bedrock of self-motivation.

But how does one find stimulation in a job where a large portion of it is mundane and repetitive?

Pink offers a useful framework. He identifies the three primary key drivers of human endeavor as *autonomy*, *mastery*, and *purpose*.[2] When these three attributes are present and in sync, superior performance is a natural consequence—the human spirit of an employee is ignited. These internal drivers allowed to flourish in any human activity—work-related or otherwise—engage one's human spirit. Human spirit is nourished through self-expression, fulfillment and personal development, and self-determination. For a minority of people, work gives expression to these things. But for most, there is no real connection between human spirit and work—it is out of reach, but not unattainable.

Let's take a closer look at autonomy, mastery, and purpose, and some practical implications.

Autonomy

Autonomy is mastering one's own destiny. Human beings naturally feel comfortable when they can make their own decisions, choose their priorities, and develop their own approaches. But the way work is organized and structured flies in the face of these natural human inclinations. As discussed, work is characterized by directing, controlling, monitoring, evaluating, and planning processes, procedures, and systems.

People want to be lead, but not controlled. Self-direction involves having choices, weighing options, and exercising freedom to decide on courses-of-action. With the need to be adaptable and agile, there's more latitude now than in the past for employees to exercise greater autonomy in deciding what needs to be done, how it's to be done, and even, when it ought to be done.

Autonomy at work can be expressed in four ways. Dan Pink refers to the four T's around autonomy:

- task,
- time,
- technique, and
- team.[3]

Task refers to the freedom to decide one's priorities. *Time* is the decision on how much—or how little—time to apply to each task; in other words, having the freedom to set deadlines. *Technique* means the liberty to decide how a task ought to be done. And *team* is selecting who to collaborate with to undertake the task. It's a simple, comprehensive model that serves as a useful framework for the application of autonomy in the workplace.

Mastery

Mastery is the innate desire to improve. Workplaces have a checklist mentality; they're places with copious amounts of compliance and system adherence. As such, there's not much scope for personal growth and development. As Pink eloquently puts it, compliance "might get you through the day, but only (engagement) will get you through the night."[4] Engagement and mastery go together.

Specialization and homogenization of work stifles personal development. People are coaxed into submissively following systems, processes, and procedures. This compliance requirement limits mastery to only a few rudimentary tasks and activities. Flexibly deploying a skills-set to a range of projects and situations is an often-untapped way of broadening developmental opportunities.

Purpose

Purpose is the pursuit of something bigger than one's self; it's a cause—a driving force. As Pink rightly says, "The most deeply motivated people—not to mention those who are more productive and satisfied—hitch their desires to a cause larger than themselves."[5] Renowned management guru, Gary Hamel challenges management to consider human spirit as a motivational force:

> The goals of management are usually described in words like 'efficiency,' 'advantage,' 'value,' 'superiority,' 'focus,' and 'differentiation.' Important as these objectives are, they lack the power to rouse human hearts.[6]

Business leaders, Gary Hamel goes on to say, "must find ways to infuse mundane business activities with deeper, soul-stirring ideals, such as honor, truth, love, justice, and beauty. Humanize what people say and you may well humanize what they do."[7] It's in our blood to seek purpose in life. This is what Dave and Wendy Ulrich refer to as the *why* of work and what Simon Sinek covers in his popular book: *Start with Why*.[8]

Leaders don't spend enough time engaging team members in developmental conversations. Conversations are the underutilized and underestimated vehicle for personal development. Leaders should take time to explain to team members the overriding purpose of the tasks, projects, or activities that need to be accomplished. What's more, when asking someone to complete any task—regardless of how routine or trivial it is—the leader should explain the consequences of doing (and not doing) the job well. Leaders shouldn't make the mistake of assuming people automatically grasp the implications of the work they do. Job-holders can't often see further than the looming task-at-hand.

Communicating purpose can be done several ways. It can involve sharing positive (or negative) customer feedback, for instance. Or purpose can be communicated by sharing how the end-user benefits from the company's product or service. Leaders don't bother communicating purpose for two reasons: First, it takes time and second, it's assumed the employee already *gets it*. People working in certain industries, such as the not-for-profit sector, have undoubtedly an easier time appreciating the connection between their work and its benefits for the community. But with a little thought and a conversation explaining the overriding purpose, leaders can provide employees with a context for the work they do. By explaining the higher purpose of work, the leader fashions the right environment for human spirit to flourish.

This brings us to the end of Chap. 2. Satisfying employees with extrinsic rewards for the work they do has merit, but it's only part of a bigger motivational landscape. Stirring the human spirit and better performance come with how work is structured and explained. The longstanding management myth that the carrot and stick is the best way to stimulate work performance needs to be put to bed. Energy engendering human spirit in work is often bypassed in the belief that it isn't attainable.

There are certain conditions that foster intrinsic motivation. We covered three. They include the freedom and autonomy to make work decisions; offering opportunities to grow and develop; and communicating the true purpose of a task or activity. As Pink reminds us, "we have a deep-seated desire to direct our own lives, to extend and expand our abilities, and live a life of purpose."[9] The authentic workplace cultivates these fundamentals.

In the next chapter, we explore the concept of workplace dignity and its connection to authentic conversation.

The Top 10 Key Points …

1. With the mindboggling transformations in the world and the rise of the knowledge worker, there's a rekindling of enthusiasm for finding meaning in work.
2. Human spirit and work is the immersion of one's human spirit in their work role.
3. Superior performance is a natural consequence of stimulating intrinsic motivation in employees; there are three ways of doing this: autonomy, mastery, and purpose.
4. Autonomy is mastering one's own destiny.
5. People want to be led, but not controlled. Self-direction involves having choices, weighing options, and exercising the freedom to decide on courses-of-action.
6. Mastery is the innate desire to improve.
7. Flexibly deploying a skills-set across a range of situations and circumstances is a way of opening developmental opportunities.

8. Purpose is the pursuit of something bigger than ourselves; it's a cause; a driving force.
9. It's natural to seek purpose in life.
10. Satisfying employees with extrinsic rewards for the work they do is important, but only part of a bigger motivational landscape.

Notes

1. https://en.wikipedia.org/wiki/Human_relations_movement.
2. Pink, D.H. (2009). Drive: The surprising truth about what motivates us. USA: Riverhead Books.
3. Ibid.
4. Ibid.
5. Ibid.
6. Hamel, G. (2009). Moon shots for management, *Harvard Business Review*, 87, 91–98.
7. Ibid.
8. Sinek, S. (2009). Start with why. New York: Penguin.
9. Pink, D.H. (2009). Drive: The surprising truth about what motivates us. USA: Riverhead Books.

3

The Concept of Workplace Dignity

We need to bring the human being back to work.

Two engineers, Donald and Jeremy, were working as part of a large, complex, multi-disciplinary project team. Twenty-five engineers were assigned to this project team. Like many large-scale projects, it came with significant budgetary and time pressures. Tempers at times would fray.

Donald had an ax to grind with Jeremy. These two engineers sat facing each other in an open-plan office. They sit less than two meters from each other. The only thing separating them was a partition. Although they couldn't see each other, they could hear each other's conversations on the phone and in person.

Donald—who was particularly unhappy with what he thought was shoddy work—decided to fire off an email to Jeremy. He explained precisely what he was upset with in the work Jeremy was producing; he didn't hold back! Before hitting the send button, Donald decided it would be a good idea to copy in the other 23 members of the project team. After all, Donald rationalized—the rest of the project team needed to know what's happening. He hit the send button.

Big mistake.

Can you guess what happened next? I bet you can.

Jeremy was furious and for a good while everyone in the office thought that World War III had broken out. Lots of shouting and finger pointing took place. Donald's actions—irrespective of whether they were justified—damaged morale, diminished trust levels to zero, and reduced productivity in that office that day, and for a considerable period after. It was disastrous.

Instead of having a conversation—as difficult as it no doubt would have been—Donald did what millions of people around the world do every single day. People use technology—whether email or something else—instead of having a face-to-face conversation in circumstances where it's possible and needed.

Why aren't we having more conversations in the workplace? Is it because we find it easier to send an electronic message? Is there a connection between the kind of communication we have (or don't have) in the workplace and the level of respect and dignity we experience? If so, what's the link between communication and dignity?

We've considered the concept of human spirit and work in Chap. 2. As I said, it's time for fresh thinking about engagement and work. We did cover three ways to foster human spirit at work. This motivational environment is not created by technology—it's created through one-to-one conversation. Leaders need to have more conversations. Conversations form the foundation of the authentic workplace.

I often wonder if the benefits of authentic conversation were more apparent, would we see more leaders indulging in more conversations in their busy places of work? I think so.

Anyway, there's a lack of quality conversations taking place in most workplaces. There's plenty of evidence to bear this out. You probably appreciate this from your own observations. There's probably enough task-specific conversations occurring in the workplace—I'm willing to concede that.

By *task-specific*, I mean conversations directly about tasks necessary in the business: sales tasks, administrative tasks, marketing tasks, operational tasks, and so on.

It's the other kind of conversations—non-task-specific—or *people-specific*—that are being neglected. Non-task-specific conversations refer to the individual, not the specific work tasks they do. They're typically referred to as developmental conversations. Developmental conversations are used to improve overall performance; they cover a host of topics. Developmental conversations are not counseling, although occasionally they may encroach on that territory.

Many conversations in the workplace are of course a hybrid of task- and non-task. For example, the delegation conversation (see Chap. 9) is usually about a task that needs to be done. However, the delegation act itself isn't generally considered a conversation; that is, a two-way dialog. It's usually thought of as a set of instructions from a manager to a team member to get a job done. For best effect, however, it ought to be a dialog, rather than a monolog. In practice, this means that the person being delegated to ought to be able to ask questions, make suggestions, seek clarification, and generally be a participant in the interaction. Apart from getting a task done, the delegation conversation—done in the right spirit—is about developing the person. So, this, like other conversations, is a mix of task and non-task elements.

Consider another example: the encouraging conversation (see Chap. 13). Although not necessarily task-specific, as its name implies, it could involve inspiring an employee about a task they are undertaking. The purpose of the encouraging conversation is reassurance; the leader believes in a team member's capacity to deliver on a project or complete a task. Like delegation, encouragement is best in dialog. The goal is to encourage someone to do (or not do) something work-related. It shouldn't be a pep-talk; it's a genuine interaction between two or more people. Nevertheless, it's another example of a conversation that can be both task- and people-specific.

Anyway, I repeat, leaders aren't having enough developmental conversations. A workplace with an absence of authentic, developmental conversations is dehumanizing. These conversation-starved workplaces are too focused on getting tasks done and place little or no emphasis on developing the people who carry out the tasks. These task-focused places of work are ironically characterized by poor task execution.

Getting back to one of the questions I asked earlier: What's the link between communication and dignity?

Workplace Dignity

One way of conceptualizing the humanization of the workplace is to consider the idea of *workplace dignity*. Kristen Lucas, who recently wrote a paper entitled *Workplace Dignity*, defines dignity as

> a personal sense of worth, value, respect, or esteem that is derived from one's humanity and individual social position; as well as being treated respectfully by others.[1]

Since most of us spend roughly a third of our adult life in a workplace, it's reasonable to expect and experience workplace dignity, consistent with Lucas' definition. Yet, this isn't the case for many people.

The traditional employment relationship, where the boss issues instructions or directives to their subordinates, is at odds with the notion of workplace dignity. Although the employment relationship is currently undergoing significant upheaval and transformation, the master/servant mind-set is still alive in many workplaces. Trade unions, rising education levels, and other factors have, to some extent, tempered workplace indignity. But we still have a long road to travel.

Arising from the employment relationship, there are several factors threatening dignity at work. Consider three. Employees are often requested to do more than is reasonably expected of them. Overwork is a form of indignity, particularly when it occurs with management support. This of course is not uncommon in times of budget constraints, cost-cutting, and frugality, for instance. Being overworked occasionally is something we all expect, as part of any job. But incessantly being overloaded is ignominious.

A manager abusing their power and authority is another common stimulus for indignity. Using idle threats and practicing intimidation is humiliating to the recipient, for instance. To be able to threaten and intimidate is an abuse of power. The person on the receiving end of this psychological bullying from their boss has little recourse, without taking a career risk.

Being micromanaged and smothering one's autonomy can be another form of humiliation for the employee. Micromanagement intrudes upon people's self-sufficiency to make decisions. The controlling manager justifies their management style with comments such as, *if I don't make the decision, nothing will happen, or the wrong decision will be made*. But a manager can be too hands-on, like peeling dried glue from their hands.

Besides these three common suspects, based on the unequal power relationship, there are myriad other forms of indignity in the world of work.

Workplace dignity is closely related to the quality of interaction and patterns of communication between manager and team member. There are countless instances of human dignity violations arising from rude and disrespectful interaction (or lack of interaction) between boss and worker. We've all witnessed, or been on the receiving end of these abuses. The connection between communication and dignity suggests that by improving the interactions between leader and team member, more respect and less humiliation will follow.

Being treated with dignity has always been important to people. But I think dignity at work is more significant to people now than ever before in industrial history for several reasons. People have a stronger desire to attain their sense of self-worth from the work they engage in now. Apart from gaining a sense of self-worth, people want to be treated with respect in all walks of life, including the workplace. There are several factors at play that make dignity at work more relevant today.

And there are some influences working against workplace dignity too. It's helpful to understand these driving and restraining forces.

First, people more than ever feel alienated from their places of work. Relentless organizational restructuring and downsizing, re-engineering, and layoffs are now commonplace. This upheaval inevitably unsettles and demoralizes employees, particularly those who lose their job! Throw into the mix the growing inequality of wages and the rising disconnect—reflected in engagement surveys results worldwide—and insecurity understandably builds. Although people feel separated from their organization more than ever, they paradoxically yearn for a more humanizing workplace. The estrangement caused by these unsettling forces present real opportunities for leaders to improve their interactions with team members.

Second, the pervasive influence of technology is another driving force to humanize work through better conversations. Isn't it ironic that we've never been more connected digitally, and yet—at a human level—we've never been so disconnected? At the click of a button, we can link with someone on the planet in seconds. This digital connectivity and the wonderful benefits it brings is a relatively recent phenomenon. In inverse proportion, there's been a rapid erosion in human connectivity. Regional communities have been replaced by virtual communities. We don't always know our neighbors, let alone the people who live in the house across the street. What's more, we're not all that interested in knowing. We keep to ourselves. We don't know the name of the person who services our car or the person behind the counter at the corner store. And yet, we humans still have a deep hunger for human connection; much deeper than 'connecting' with friends on Facebook. So, the workplace can—and does to some extent—fill this void, as our de facto community.

The workplace—despite feelings of emotional isolation—is a prime source of community. Traditional groupings for emotional bonding are evaporating. There's a decline of neighborhood, dwindling church attendance, disappearing civic groups, and less reliance on extended families, for example. Can the workplace *community*—even with its apparent insecurities—compensate for these dwindling, traditional pillars of society? For an increasing percentage of employees, the workplace—at the very least—offers the only steady link with other people—a constant source of on-going human interaction.

Third, with the digital explosion, comes lots of exposure to new ideas, philosophies, and perspectives. For instance, Eastern philosophies are no longer mysterious to Westerners. What's more, Eastern philosophies have inspired

Westerners to consider other forms of spirituality. There's a growing curiosity in *Buddhism* and *Confucianism*, for example. Zen Buddhism and Confucianism promote practices like mindfulness and meditation and emphasize values such as loyalty to one's group instead of individualism. Central to these philosophies is the discovery of one's spiritual identity in all pursuits. These sorts of ideas are finding greater acceptance and application in our society. Time-honored beliefs such as these are shaping the way we think about our lives, including the role work plays.

With a large slice of the current workforce contemplating retirement and about to depart full-time work, *baby boomers* are reflecting on the meaning of their lives and the legacy they leave behind. As aging baby boomers move closer to life's greatest certainty—death—they naturally have a growing interest in contemplating life's meaning. I know I do! This reflection concentrates more attention on one's work contribution.

Fourth, there's a lot of talk and instances of artificial intelligence taking people's jobs now and in the not-so-distant future. At the same time, escalating global competition has, in the past two decades, shifted attention from machines to people as the primary source of competitive edge. Despite this, most people—bar a select few—are increasingly being treated as a disposable commodity, regardless of their capabilities, skills-set, or educational attainment. Yet it's the technological tools that are the real commodities. Technology is easily assessable, reducing in price all the time in relative terms, and offers the customer a bewildering array of options. Technology is no longer the edge it once was. It's people who are still the differentiators in the working world.

Even though people are generally treated as a resource, high performing individuals are in great demand worldwide, across all industries. The relentless pressure of global competition has escalated the value of people's creative energy; thinking outside the box is the new black. Harnessing and maximizing people's ideas and ingenuity involves the collaboration of head and heart. Innovative thinking that translates to practice is a rich source of adaptive advantage. Innovative thinking is the fuel that drives the necessary adaptive gain in an economy characterized by accelerated change and uncertainty.

Even with these four drivers to humanize our places of work, there are factors working against this idea. The human connection to the organization is more tenuous than it ever was. Instead of a place of dignity and security, today's workplace is one of unease and insecurity. Work was once a stable and predictable pillar in one's life. But today, more and more people are changing jobs for a host of reasons every couple of years or less. High turnover accounts for some of the tension we experience in the workplace.

But most people, as I suggested in Chap. 1, want more from work than just a job. Nevertheless, the insecurity of a warp speed, transforming marketplace means people can't bank on a perspective beyond the immediate. People naturally think, *I can't afford to relax and get too comfortable; I might be made redundant tomorrow.* Yet the work-setting is the only community most of us have beyond the family. It's a bind.

With the workplace community under threat, a feeling of dignity is paramount to people. Most people have a craving for a sense of self-worth from their organizational work. They want to be treated with respect. As straightforward as that might sound, the workplace faces many challenges that blocks a sense of dignity from prevailing. Dignity is the exception, rather than the rule in most organizations, regrettably.

But it doesn't have to be this way.

The workplace can be a profound source of inspiration. People can feel they're making important contributions for themselves, their family, the organization, and society-at-large. Some occupations, such as those in the medical profession—the business of saving lives—have a clear and poignant connection between the work they do and the contribution they make. A person's sense of self-respect can come from self-actualization. Personal growth and development is one of the ways people gain a sense of dignity. Feeling part of a greater whole can be dignifying too. Knowing that one is working toward a common cause that's making a difference can be a source of self-worth. One can feel dignified with the knowledge they are contributing to something worthwhile.

Communication holds the key.

Poor communication practices in a workplace destroy dignity. Disrespectful behavior seems to be on the rise everywhere we care to look. Bullying and harassment are rife in some quarters. Education programs, policies, and legislation don't seem to deter poor behavior. With a paint by numbers approach or the mindless systematization of everything from serving a customer to applying for leave, communication at work is dumbed down. Communication gives way to following systems. It's dehumanizing. Humanness is discouraged, even frowned upon in the relentless quest for methodization.

> **Where the Rubber Meets the Road …**
>
> **The 'Faceless' Interview**
>
> I remember recently hearing a story from a very capable person applying for a relatively senior role. Jennifer told me that in a job interview—consisting of four panelists—she didn't manage to make eye contact with two on the panelists once in the entire hour-long interview! They were too busy filling out the requisite forms and paperwork. They were engaged in ticking all the boxes and filling in the form guide. Jennifer—who incidentally told me that she missed out on the position—made the comment to me that if she'd bumped into those two panelists on the street immediately after the interview, neither of them would have recognized her.
>
> People are made to feel disposable at work; even before they may get the job! Employees have a number and title—not dissimilar from a prison—they are treated as a commodity; they are classified as a human resource.

The common denominator in all forms of indignity is poor or non-existent communication. People's dignity can be affirmed or threatened by their interactions with others within and beyond the gates of the organization. So, the key to increased workplace dignity is upgrading the quality and quantity of interactions between people. More non-task or people-specific conversations are the perfect vehicle for enhancing workplace dignity.

In the next chapter, we consider the lack of authentic conversations in the workplace and how this can be changed.

The Top 10 Key Points …

1. The reality is there's a lack of quality conversations taking place in most organizational settings.
2. A workplace with an absence of authentic, developmental conversations is dehumanizing. These workplaces are focused on getting tasks done and place little or no emphasis on developing the people who carry out the tasks.
3. One way of conceptualizing the humanization of the workplace is to consider the idea of workplace dignity.
4. Dignity is defined as "a personal sense of worth, value, respect, or esteem that is derived from one's humanity and individual social position; as well as being treated respectfully by others."
5. Three roadblocks threatening dignity in the workplace include overwork, a manager abusing their power, and a manager micromanaging.

6. Workplace dignity is closely related to the quality of interaction and patterns of communication between manager and team member.
7. There are several factors at play that make dignity at work more relevant than ever.
8. While the workplace community is under threat, a feeling of dignity is important to people. Most people have a desire to gain a sense of self-worth from their organizational work and to experience being treated with respect.
9. The workplace can be a profound source of inspiration. People can feel they are making important contributions for themselves, their family, the organization, and society-at-large.
10. The common denominator in all forms of indignity is poor or non-existent communication.

Note

1. Lucas, K. (2015). "Workplace dignity: Communicating inherent, earned, and remediated dignity." *Journal of Management Studies*. 52, 5, 620–46.

4

A Lack of Authentic Conversations

Why do leaders lack the capacity or willingness to converse with those they work with? Is it a lack of skill or a lack of will, or both?

We considered some widespread evidence of poor or non-existent communication in the last chapter and its impact in the workplace. To highlight the extent of the problem of poor communication practices, consider the research. According to Deloitte's *Global Human Capital Trends* report of 2014, 79 per cent of organizations worldwide struggle to engage and retain their employees and 86 per cent believe they do not have an adequate leadership pipeline to address these problems.[1] An increasing number of management thinkers are calling for a more humane workplace; one that energizes employees by creating an environment where it feels good to come to work. People in these more positive surroundings get things done more proficiently, and business results follow.

The Deloitte's survey results—although unsurprising—are nevertheless stark. Why are managers reluctant to engage the people they lead? Why do leaders lack the capacity or willingness to converse with those they work with? Is it a lack of skill or a lack of will, or both? Just as a bad case of the flu needs medical treatment, so too does an absence of quality conversation need remedying.

Simon Mitchell in his article, *Driving Workplace Performance Through High-quality Conversations*,[2] defines the *whats* and *hows* of leadership. The 'whats' refer to the tasks leaders are supposed to do. Leaders are challenged to foster innovation, focus on customer needs, develop long-term strategies, make countless day-to-day decisions, and simultaneously, develop future talent. This list is like putting together a piece of furniture from *Ikea*—there's always more to it than meets the eye. Nonetheless, these tasks are at the heart of leadership. They are what Mitchell refers to as the *whats*.

What are the 'hows'? The *hows* are the ways leaders get the *whats* done.

The day-to-day interactions—the *hows*—determine leadership success. Communicating is how the *whats* are achieved. In Simon Mitchell's words,

Leadership outcomes will, to a large extent, depend on the dozens of conversations leaders have every day. The success of leadership will be determined by the effectiveness of these conversations.[3]

Conversation is the tool to realize the objectives of leadership. Just as following the instruction manual can be underestimated and underutilized when assembling a piece of furniture, so too can conversations be taken for granted. Leaders would do well to focus on the *hows* as much as the *whats*.

DDI's research highlights that leaders everywhere are deficient in the fundamentals of how to have effective interactions with their team members, and other colleagues.[4] This research reinforces the gulf between what leaders are required to do and how they go about doing it.

Based on findings from the actual data of thousands of leaders who have been evaluated through DDI's assessment centers, communication skills are poor or non-existent. The research underscores that both executives and junior leaders are inept at conversing. The outcome of the assessment centers found leaders to be generally poor at clarifying a situation before acting. Further, the clear majority (90 per cent) of leaders rely on their own ideas rather than seeking involvement from others. Worse still, 89 per cent of leaders failed to listen or respond to interpersonal cues from those they interact with. The findings indicated that there is often no lucidity around the steps to be taken in situations requiring some form of action. Disturbingly, only 5 per cent of leaders are effective in building trust in their interactions with team members.[5] All of this is sobering.

In DDI's previous global research in 2012, employees spoke about what they perceived as damaged self-esteem from talking with their managers. The research suggests that 60 per cent of people felt their self-esteem dented by their leader. These people claim they would rather do almost anything else than sit through a performance conversation with their boss. Although they did acknowledge that a good boss with excellent interaction skills would enhance their productivity by as much as 60 per cent!

Apart from helping people to feel good about themselves, there are undoubtedly productivity benefits to be gained from better communication skills. Improved conversations translate into more motivated and industrious employees. That's not just my view; it's the opinion of the employees surveyed too. This seemingly straight forward undertaking of talking and listening to people can make a very big difference.

Many leaders have forgotten, or perhaps never appreciated, the relevance of simply being human. Being human includes building trusting working relationships with those one works closely with. As James Kouzes and Barry Posner in their book, *Credibility* put it: "Leadership in a relationship."[6] Having a healthy working relationship requires a reasonable level of trust. It means listening to others with care and humanity. Although important, it's not as easy as it sounds.

We're all busy juggling several balls in the air. We have many interests to attend to, including our own. We get distracted. We get side-tracked. We become self-indulgent. We assume we know what the person speaking to us it going to say next and switch off and not listen. In short, we are human. But we probably also acknowledge that a little more engagement and humanity translates into more trust, just as a little more exercise translates into more energy.

Many people have been detached from humanity at work for so long, they don't even know it. We need to bring the human being back to work. There is light at the end of the long, dark tunnel. As we move to the third decade of the new millennium, there's a movement growing for a more humanized workplace. This movement, not dissimilar from the human relations drive 100 years ago reacting to the hard edges of scientific management, heralds a new era for leadership. This fresh leadership paradigm invites leaders to invest in building trusting working relationships with those they lead.[7] The best leaders do this instinctively. They understand that fostering a trusting working relationship is the bedrock for higher performance. This link between trust and high performance has currency for all leaders from boardroom to the basement.

It's only relatively recently that research has validated the connection between trust and engagement.[8] There is no doubting that a good, healthy working relationship between a manager and team member will boost engagement levels. And higher engagement levels positively impact on-the-job performance. If high engagement levels populate the entire organization, enterprise performance goes through the roof. That's an exciting thought; not to mention, possibility! As research evidence continues to mount, it is unsurprising to see a brighter spotlight on interaction between leader and team member. Now that it's established that the quality of the working relationship influences performance, there's nowhere to hide.

But even with solid evidence, the idea of the leader building collaborative relationships with their team is not as widely accepted as one might think. In some quarters, it's either not a top priority or worse—actively discouraged. The idea that it's the leader's job to be decisive, visionary, and dynamic is still propagated. Although these attributes are undeniably admirable, they take precedence over attributes such as being adaptive, agile, and collaborative.

However, a growing number of management thinkers are sprouting the wisdom that building trusting relationships is the leader's primary responsibility. I would suggest to you this: Everything else done in the workplace hangs off solid working relationship. Trust, dignity, and authenticity is the glue for the edifice of leadership. Without these qualities, managers must work doubly hard to achieve the results they're paid to get. Without trust, people second guess the leader's motives; there's a lack of respect for the leader's opinions. People default to playing safe. They search for hidden meaning in the words the leader utters. Tasks take longer, quality suffers, and the leader's influence diminishes. People do things because they must, not because they want to.

Authentic Conversations

Building trust, demonstrating dignity, and increasing engagement begins with authentic conversations. There are other ways to show trust (and lose it too!) and dignity. But it is nurtured one-on-one. It starts with the conversation—one authentic conversation, followed by another, and so on.

Technology has got in the way of the conversation, according to Nigel Purse from the *Oxford Group*:

> Throughout human history, people have talked to each other—using gesture and touch, smiles and frowns, myths and stories—to build collaboration and trust and get things done. Somehow in today's world of technology, email, social media, remote working and globalization, we have forgotten this simple truth.[9]

Whether you're introvert or extravert, a technical expert or generalist, task-focused or people-focused, senior or junior manager, educated or not educated, young or old, you can strengthen relationships with your work colleagues. Step one is to start conversing. Build into your weekly schedule short, purposeful one-on-one conversations with your team members. It's like investing your money wisely; it seems like an imposition initially, but over time it pays off exponentially.

You don't need the gift of the gab or be a brilliant conversationalist. Just start. If you go into each conversation with the genuine intention to more deeply understand your colleague, show care and stewardship, and provide support and encouragement, that's enough. I'll help you with context, content, and process as we journey through the pages of this book.

As I've said, there aren't enough authentic, developmental, or performance conversations happening in the workplace. You'd be hard pressed to find any leader who felt they were having too many developmental or performance conversations. Anyway, it's not about keeping score. Creating a conversation culture is an incremental process. Conversations build upon one another. They go off in different directions, sometimes without warning. Thoughts and ideas are expounded. Some comments and statements fall on deaf ears; others are ignored. One way of looking at dialog is that your interaction with a team member is one long conversation, punctuated by interruptions. When you meet again, you both pick up the threads of the previous dialog. Comments like, *Last time we spoke, I recall you saying ... Remember when you made the point that ...* bridge the time and space between now and the previous conversation.

Conversation skills training does help. But—like so many things in life—practice makes perfect. By indulging in regular, meaningful conversations, confidence grows, and skill levels improve. Sometimes having training for conversations—or anything else for that matter—is a credible way of postponing what ought to be done—now. In this case, it's practicing having authentic conversations. The exercise of having actual authentic conversations is the training. People make excuses like, *we can't start having developmental conversations until we're 'trained.'* Start anyway. Start now. Training will enrich the practice. Training can be a useful supplement, but it's not a cure-all.

I think we rely too much on training. But isn't learning and development important, I hear you ask? Yes, it is. Training has limitations though. You can't, for instance, train people to be authentic. One can be highly skilled at conducting conversations, but lack authenticity. Likewise, one can be authentic, but without necessarily being mechanically skillful at conversations. Given a choice, you'll get a better outcome being authentic with limited skill than vice versa—that is, a highly skilled conversationalist, with zero authenticity. Skills training can, however, provide a process that may lead to greater authenticity. We'll cover five attributes of authentic conversations in the next two chapters.

So how do you *make* people authentic? You can't. You can give people guidelines that assist with authenticity; but the rest is up to them. Being authentic is a choice; it's an attitude; it's not a skill or competency. You're either authentic, or you're not. It's a state-of-mind. If a leader demonstrates authenticity in their dealings with others, it tends to be reciprocated; not always, of course. But on many occasions, it does. It works in reverse too. A leader who is inauthentic is inviting the people they interact with to be artificial too. A leader's attitude sets the tone of communication.

High performing organizations have several things in common. One of these characteristics is the presence of authentic communication. People mostly feel safe to speak their mind in these high-performance environments. There's a willingness to be open to constructive criticism. Communication is clear, transparent, conversational, and proactive. People are encouraged to speak up formally in meetings and informally in the corridor. Developmental conversations are commonplace; they are constructive, outcome-driven, and respectful. Conversations are proactive and occur when they should, with who they should, and not only because of something's going wrong.

People generally want to know how their work fits into the bigger landscape. They want to know how they're tracking. Where needed, people want to be coached, not directed. Authentic, timely, and relevant conversations is the tool of trade to meet these fundamental human needs. Incredible benefits can be gained with minimum effort.

Kim Janson in her article, *Conversations that Unleash Employee Talent*[10] has a useful model for conversations that covers most contingencies and answers five basis questions:

- What do I need to do?
- How am I doing?
- How did I go?
- How will I benefit?
- How do I grow and develop?

People want to know precisely what's expected of them in their work role (or anywhere else, for that matter). They want to know if they are on track. And if not, how to get back on track. Ultimately, after completing a task or project, or undertaking some personal development, they benefit from a review of their experience. They appreciate knowing what's in it for them in accomplishing a task. And they generally want to know how they can grow, develop, and improve. A leader can address these questions by applying Janson's model.

A little over a quarter of a century ago, there was a significant shift in management thinking. It entailed a movement away from *command and control* to *empowerment and collaboration*. The change emphasized the leader as coach.[11] I like Angie Dixey's summation that "coaching should be a way of managing, rather than a prescribed activity."[12] Looking back, it has been a long and painful evolution. The shift from the leader being the authority to the leader being the coach is still playing out. Traditional management thinking is deeply-rooted, like the 100-year-old oak tree.

In Chap. 5, we introduce the *Five Pillars of Authentic Communication Framework* and cover the first two pillars—*Establish a trusting relationship* and *Agree on expectations*.

The Top 10 Key Points …

1. According to Deloitte's *Global Human Capital Trends* report of 2014, 79 per cent of organizations worldwide struggle to engage and retain their employees and 86 per cent believe they do not have an adequate leadership pipeline to address these problems.
2. Conversation is the vehicle to achieve the objectives of leadership.
3. DDI's research highlights that leaders around the world are lacking in the vital skills needed to have effective interactions with team members and other colleagues.
4. There are clearly enormous productivity benefits to be gained from improving the quality of leaders' ability to interact in the workplace.
5. Many leaders have forgotten, or perhaps never appreciated, the relevance of simply being human in their interactions with others.
6. A link between trust and employee engagement has only recently been proven through research.
7. Even with more awareness and solid evidence, the notion of the leader working proactively building better working relationships with their team members is not yet widely accepted.
8. By indulging in regular, meaningful conversations, confidence grows, and skill expands and deepens.
9. Being authentic is a choice; it's an attitude; it's not a skill or competency. You're either authentic, or you're not.
10. A little over a quarter of a century ago, there was a significant shift in management thinking. It entailed a movement away from command and control to empowerment and collaboration.

Notes

1. Somos, A. (2014). Humanize your workplace: 5 tips to improve the employee "lived experience." *Leadership Excellence*, 31, 6, 12.
2. Mitchell, S. (2014). Driving workplace performance through high-quality conversations. *Strategic HR Review*, 31, 1, 42–44.
3. Ibid.
4. Ibid.
5. Ibid.
6. Kouzes, J.M. & Posner, B.Z. (2011). Credibility: How leaders gain and lose It, why people demand it (2nd ed.). Jossey-Bass.
7. Purse, N. (2015). The 5 conversations that really matter in business: Transforming trust, engagement and performance at work. *Development and Learning in Organizations*, 29, 4, 3–5.
8. Gallup (2013). "State of the global workplace report," available at www.gallup.com/services/178517/state-global-workplace.aspx (accessed 3rd of May 2016).
9. Ibid.
10. Janson, K. (2015). Conversations that unleash employee talent. *The Journal of Quality and Participation*, 38, 1, 23–28.
11. Evered, R.D. & Selman, J.C. (1989). Coaching and the art of management. *Organizational Dynamics*, 18(2), 16–32.
12. Dixey, A. (2015). Managerial coaching: A formal process or a daily conversation? *International Journal of Evidence Based Coaching and Mentoring*, 9, 77–89.

5

Two Task-focused Pillars of Authentic Conversations

Authenticity is the new emotional intelligence.

Craig was about to start a performance conversation with Mary, one of his supervisors. He had arranged to meet Mary in a quiet, comfortable room away from his office.

Craig had frequently been told—and had witnessed several times first-hand—about the abrupt way in which Mary spoke to her team members when she wanted something done. Craig felt that this was an aspect of Mary's communication that required improvement.

Mary was inclined to tell people what to do, rather than ask them. Her team naturally resented this. Craig was worried that Mary might not accept this criticism constructively. He was understandably a little apprehensive about this conversation.

Mary arrived punctually, and Craig started with a question, "Mary, you've no doubt had a chance to review your current role. If there is one area of communication you believe is an opportunity for growth, what is it?" After a lengthy and awkward pause, she replied, "I can't seem to get my team members to show any initiative. I have to do all the thinking for them."

"Okay. Can you elaborate on this so that I understand what you mean?" "Well, I find myself telling people what to do when I'd rather they show initiative and do what they are paid to do." "What do you think the reason for this is, Mary?" "I don't really know."

"What are the consequences of this?" probed Craig. "Well, I find I must raise my voice and direct people to do what they should know already," Mary responded in an agitated voice. "When you raise your voice, what happens?" "People walk off in

a huff usually and don't listen to me." "I see. I guess you're not happy about this reaction, then?" "No, I'm not."

"What would you like to happen?" "I would like them to listen to me and just do what needs to be done without any argument" "Well, what can you do differently to get this result?" "I don't really know."

"Have you tried asking them without raising your voice?" Craig suggested. "Yeah, but that doesn't work." "When was the last time you did this?" "I can't remember. I get so frustrated I can't help raising my voice." "But you say that's not working," Craig replied patiently. "No, it definitely doesn't work, but it's the only way."

"Can I suggest you try asking them in a calm manner and see what happens? It's worth a go, isn't it?" "Well, nothing else is working, Craig!" Mary responded, exasperated.

"So, I have your commitment to give it another try?" "Yeah, I suppose so," sighed Mary.

"Is there anything I can do to help?" "No, not really. You've been helpful just listening to me. I'll just have to control myself and do as you suggest." "Good. Come back and tell me how you get on, won't you?"[1]

In the previous chapter I signaled the limitations of classroom learning to improve conversation quality. Theoretical training can undoubtedly be a worthwhile adjunct. But practice and reflection are the best learning devices when it comes to conversations. It's questionable whether you can learn to be authentic in the classroom, for instance. Authenticity is a way of thinking rather than a technique. There are five traits—or what I refer to as pillars—of authentic work-related conversations. They originate with the right attitude, like most things in life.

I'll cover two of these pillars later in this chapter and three more in Chap. 6. The two pillars I cover here are task-focused and the three I consider in the next chapter are people-focused. You might recall that I discussed two dimensions—task- and people-focus in the last chapter.

But first, what's meant by this word—*authenticity*, particularly when it comes to conversation? "Authenticity is the new emotional intelligence," according to the human resources manager of *Hampshire County Council*.[2] I like that. A recent survey indicates that trust and transparency are more important to the reputation of a business than the quality of the products and services.[3] Jill Morin, in her thought-provoking article, *Better Make It Real: Defining and Expressing Organizational Authenticity*, believes that authenticity happens when organizations walk their talk. It is revealed moment by moment, through the experiences provided to stakeholders—employees, customers, vendors, suppliers, and other key business partners. When organizations are who they say they are and do what they say they do, they (can) thrive, in part because they differentiate themselves from the rest of the "us too" pack. The authenticity of any enterprise ... begins with its leaders.[4]

If authenticity is an attitude, then there are two parts to this. First, authenticity has to do with the mindset of the participants in the conversation. How prepared are people to be authentic in each conversation? Are they ready to be open with each other? Are they in the right frame-of-mind to say what needs to be said? Are they willing to show respect to one another? People's attitude shapes their preparedness to be authentic. A conversationalist's attitude hinges on countless factors, including the circumstances leading to the conversation. Attitude is the starting point.

Attitude governs behavior. And it's the actions that make up the second part of authentic interaction. Certain actions or inactions will amplify or lessen authenticity. The five pillars of authentic conversation I'm about to share with you are a combination of attitude and behavior.

These five pillars are the foundations for authentic conversations. Each pillar isn't necessarily a conversation on its own. Although you'll find some correlation between the five pillars and the 10 conversations we cover later in Parts II and III. The *relationship building conversation* (see Chap. 15), for instance, has a strong connection with *establish a trusting relationship*—the third pillar. The *encouraging conversation* (see Chap. 13) draws heavily on the fourth pillar—*show genuine appreciation*. And the *visioning conversation* (see Chap. 11) has much in common with the fifth pillar—*build for the future*. Despite these similarities, the process of effective dialog between two people over time needs to address all five pillars for authentic interaction between leader and team member.

Let's look at the framework illustrated in Fig. 5.1. I'll then explain how each of these pillars contributes to an atmosphere of authenticity. Some of these pillars, for a variety of reasons, are easier to do than others. People's personalities and the history and chemistry between people are factors that impact on the degree of difficulty. The quality of the working relationship, nonetheless, is improved when all five pillars are evident in the continuous dialog. The reverse is true too: The quality of the working relationship will certainly deteriorate if these attributes are not addressed.

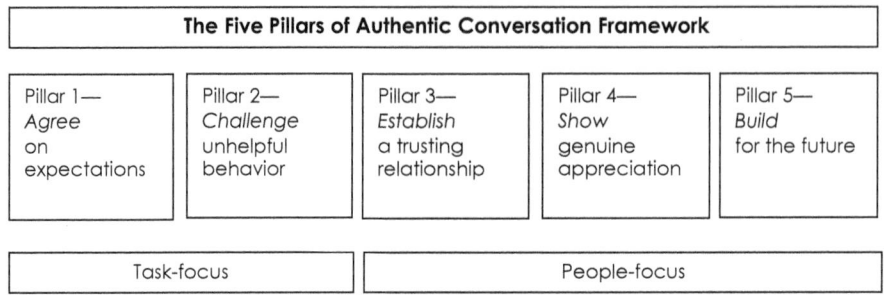

Fig. 5.1 The five pillars of authentic conversation

The pillars shown in Fig 5.1 are in no order. Like a row of pillars holding up a roof, they all have a role to play. Pillars 1 and 2 are mainly task-related (Chap. 5) and Pillars 3, 4, and 5 are mostly people-related (Chap. 6), as I mentioned earlier.

Pillar 1: Agree on Expectations

Agreeing on expectations sounds simple, doesn't it? But it's not. To achieve alignment between the leader and team member, five questions need to be answered. The questions are:

1. Does the leader know what the expectations of the team member are?
2. Has the leader communicated their standards clearly to the team member?
3. Does the team member understand and accept the leader's expectations?
4. Has the leader gained the commitment of the team member to consistently meet those standards?
5. Has the leader provided the right supportive environment for the team member to meet expectations?

Leaders need to firstly be clear in their own mind about their expectation of others in their work area. Once they have determined what these performance standards are, the leader needs to communicate them to their team clearly and comprehensively. It's one thing to understand a leader's expectation, and another, for a follower to accept and commit to it. The leader needs to know—and not just assume—that their team is committed to meeting their standards on a consistent basis. And finally, the leader should remove any roadblocks and create a supportive environment to permit these standards to be met. Agreeing on expectations is quite complex.

I want to elaborate on these five questions more fully.

Does the leader know what their expectations of the team member are? is the first step in the process of agreeing on expectations. A leader must be crystal clear in their mind about what they expect from others. What is the minimum acceptable standard of performance you will tolerate? What is unacceptable? What are the behaviors and actions that exceed your expectations? Questions such as these seem simple enough. But it's more difficult to answer these questions than it may first appear.

Imagine you are delegating the organization of a management retreat to a team member, for example. This team member is required to book the rooms, organize the venue, coordinate the speakers, compile the agenda, and so on. What are your expectations for these tasks?

The key for a project such as this is to break it down into component parts, that is, agenda, accommodation, speakers, venue, and so on. By breaking down the project into smaller chunks, you can consider your expectations for each lump of activity. For the agenda, your hope is to maximize the participation of attendees to foster collaboration, for example.

Once the leader is clear about their expectation, the next challenge is to communicate that standard. One of the most effective ways of communicating a standard is by illustrating it with a critical incident. This puts the expectation into context; it can be explained in practical terms. Here is what you might say to the organizer of the retreat:

> I want this meeting to be totally participatory; I want everyone in the room to feel they have an opportunity to contribute. This would be achieved in my opinion if most of the discussion is originated from the audience, and not the speakers. Do you remember last year's retreat: Everyone was totally engaged?

The organizer now has a picture of what success looks like.

Once the expectation has been communicated, is it understood and accepted? It's often mistakenly assumed that an outcome is clear and understood, when in fact it isn't. To help, the leader needs to ask two questions. First: *Are you clear on what I expect?* The leader needs to pause long enough for the other person to nod, grunt, or affirm with a *yes*. If not, it invites the other person to clarify or ask questions. The second question should be along the lines of: *Is this a fair and reasonable expectation in your opinion?* Again, the leader looks for a signal of positive affirmation before plowing on.

Getting back to my earlier example of organizing the retreat, the person this has been delegated to must feel comfortable with meeting your expectations. If, after all, they're sitting there thinking this is an absurd request, that is, it's unattainable, likely, it won't be met. Taking the time to ask these couple of questions significantly improves the prospects of your expectation being met.

Once expectations have been clarified and agreed, the next step is to gain a sense of commitment. It's again common for the leader to assume the other person is automatically dedicated to meeting the standard. And later—when the expectation hasn't been met—the leader is surprised and disappointed.

If there's no commitment, it's very likely that the task will either not get done or—more likely—get done in a sub-standard way. Gaining commitment simply means asking for assurance. *Can I get your commitment to achieve this the way we've discussed?* is a simple, but deceptively powerful question to ask? Again, the leader wants either a nod, grunt, or preferably, a *yes*. This affirms commitment. Often, with this affirmation, the other person will follow through; they don't want to let their boss down. Conversely, if the leader assumes they have the other person's commitment, they can be sadly let down.

The final question is: *Have I provided the right supportive environment for others to meet expectations?* The leader doesn't always consider their supportive role either. A 'supportive environment' could mean the authority to make decisions, the right skills for the task, access to information and resources to help, a realistic time-frame, links to people that can help get the job done, or many other considerations. If the time-frame is unrealistic, for example, then it will impact on standards and possibly weaken the commitment to carry out the job. This—and other support measures—need considering and discussing.

In sum, the leader can get agreement on expectations and add a significant degree of legitimacy to the conversation by covering these five questions.

Pillar 2: Challenge Unhelpful Behavior

Unhelpful behavior can be classified two ways. One type of behavior is a one-off incident without precedent. Although unique, the incident is still significant enough to warrant the leader's attention. Events like this could be an uncharacteristic outburst in the office that upsets several people, for example. Or it could be someone losing their cool over the telephone with a customer. Or it might be a failure to communicate vital information in a timely manner to a colleague. This communication lapse could seriously hamper the colleague from doing their job properly. Although these are not necessarily regular incidents, they are nevertheless obstructive.

The second type of unhelpful behavior is repetitive. The same themes occur; for example, it could involve excessive negativity in meetings. Or it might be apparent sexist behavior, such as inappropriate jokes being told in the office.

Or it could be continual tardiness; being perpetually late submitting work past set deadlines. In these cases, a track record is perhaps forming, and the habit needs breaking.

Whether one-off or on-going, the leader should sit down with the offender and discuss the behavior with a view of remedying it. Large, one-off incidents or regular unhelpful patterns of behavior are best tackled ASAP. The longer unhelpful conduct is avoided, the harder it is to change the behavior.

Leaders often fail to challenge unhelpful behavior for a variety of reasons. They may rationalize that it's better to let sleeping dogs lie, or it will aggravate things further, or open a can of worms. But these reasons aren't usually valid and potentially problematic sooner or later. With no feedback, the person exhibiting unhelpful behavior isn't deterred from carrying on as usual. No feedback from their manager may even implicitly encourage more unhelpful behavior. While the person in question is oblivious to the negative impact of their conduct, the leader becomes increasingly exasperated. Not challenging obstructive action (or inaction) is inauthentic. How? Because it's not uncommon for a manager to take their pent-up frustration out on the person indirectly, or at least not honestly, via feedback.

When difficult behavior begins to adversely affect the workplace, the leader must step in. But I'm sure you appreciate that it's not so simple. The fear of confronting someone with poor conduct—and the anticipated reaction of the culprit—can deter a manager from initiating that challenging conversation. Fear gets in the way.

The fear stems from a lack of confidence to adequately handle the situation. Or, the perceived prospect of damaging—or further damaging—the fabric of the working relationship could stop managers from taking the next step. The bottom line: The leader doesn't want to offend the other person.

Even with oodles of courage, a manager can balk, not knowing how to have the right conversation, in the right way. The dilemma for the inexperienced manager is not only what to say, but also, what not to say. This indecisiveness adds another layer of reluctance to act, notwithstanding their pluck in wanting to act. The leader knows, however, that they have a responsibility to act. But they may be also paralyzed by fear and elect to not follow through with a conversation. This emotional turmoil compounds matters further. The leader may feel guilty and inadequate, simultaneously.

At the other end of the spectrum, some managers just dive straight in, regardless of the consequences. They let their emotions get the better of them. Their frustration is overwhelming. They let fly. The intended 'conversation' quickly turns into a reprimand. Instead of seeking out the causes of the behavior, the conversation ends up as a full-blown confrontation.

It's not just the words used, but the regulation of emotions that become important in these situations. Acknowledging their inner state is a good place for the leader to start. *How am I feeling? And why am I feeling this way?* are constructive questions to ask oneself before launching in like a hungry person at a smorgasbord dinner.

A second important non-verbal trait is empathy; that is, the ability to listen non-judgmentally. Empathy is the experience of understanding another person's perspective. It's one of the hallmarks of emotional intelligence. You put yourself in their shoes and feel what the other's person is feeling.[5] Understanding the other person's position—by the way—doesn't mean agreeing with their opinion. Empathy means being able to affirm another perspective.

Why then is challenging unhelpful behavior a pillar of authentic conversations? It's authentic because these matters are brought out in the open—they are put on the table for discussion. It's not something that goes unspoken. When a leader initiates these sometimes-awkward conversations, the offending person knows where they stand. This adds an important layer of authenticity to the working relationships.

We've considered the first two of five pillars in the framework; they are related specifically to work tasks—agreeing on expectations and challenging unhelpful behavior.

In the next chapter, we tackle the other three people-focused pillars of authentic conversations.

The Top 10 Key Points …

1. The Five Pillars of Authentic Conversation Framework consist of two task-focused pillars: agree on expectations and challenge unhelpful behavior.
2. There are five questions a leader needs to consider for Pillar 1—Agree on expectations. The first question is: Does the leader know what their expectations of the team member are?
3. The second question is: Has the leader communicated their standards clearly to the team member?
4. The third question is: Does the team member understand and accept the leader's expectations?
5. The fourth question is: Has the leader gained the commitment of the team member to consistently meet those standards?

6. And the fifth question is: Has the leader provided the right supportive environment for the team member to meet expectations?
7. In terms of Pillar 2—Challenging unhelpful behavior—there are two types of behavior: one-off incidents and repetitive behavior.
8. Whether one-off or repetitive, the leader should sit down with the offender and discuss the behavior with a view of remedying it as soon as possible.
9. The leader's fear of challenging unhelpful behavior can stem from a lack of confidence in their ability to adequately handle the situation.
10. Challenging unhelpful behavior is a pillar of authentic conversations because these matters are being discussed in the open.

Notes

1. Baker, T.B. (2013). The end of the performance review: A new approach to appraising employee performance. London: Palgrave Macmillan.
2. CIPD (2012). Where has all the trust gone? London, *Chartered Institute of Personnel and Development* retrieved from http://www.trustinorganizations.com/Resources/Documents/WhereHasAllTheTrustGone.pdf.pdf.
3. Morin, J.J. (2011). Better make it real: Defining and expressing organizational authenticity. *Leader to Leader*, 61, 12–16.
4. Ibid.
5. https://www.psychologytoday.com/basics/empathy.

6

Three People-focused Pillars of Authentic Conversations

The prosperity of all enterprises is dependent upon the growth of the people working in it.

In this final chapter of Part I, I review the three other pillars of the authentic conversations framework. These pillars include *Establish a trusting relationship*, *Show genuine appreciation*, and *Challenge unhelpful behavior*. These are the people-focused dimensions of the framework.

Pillar 3: Establish a Trusting Relationship

Trust and authenticity are related, like brother and sister. Authentic communicating builds trust. We humans have a good bullshit detector; we can sense authenticity and inauthenticity reasonably quickly and effortlessly. Having an authentic attitude and approach essentially means contributing openly and trustingly. A lack of trust, on the other hand, leads to superficiality and cautiousness. The interaction is guarded, shallow, and averting genuineness and openness. Being trusting is like the glue in a collage; it holds everything together.

What then can a leader do (or not do) that can establish and maintain a trusting working relationship? There's a multitude of issues that affect trust levels between people. There are four key elements I suggest you concentrate on:

- Treat people fairly.
- Recognize their positive contributions.
- Give people clear direction.
- Support their development.

We'll look at each of these fundamentals in more depth shortly.

According to Joseph McManus and Joseph Mosca in their article, *Strategies to Build Trust and Improve Employee Engagement,*

> Trust generally involves the willingness to be vulnerable to the actions of another based on the belief that this other actor will perform as expected, even if you cannot monitor their behavior.[1]

It's unsurprising that when a leader exhibits this trait, people perform better, are more satisfied, become engaged, demonstrate loyalty, and are open to change.

Heightened trust is also a precondition for innovation and continuous improvement. It stands to reason that people aren't going to risk trying a new approach, unless they're confident they have the backing and trust of their boss. Trust, to a changing work environment, is like high octane fuel for a racing car.

Consider the public and not-for-profit sectors, for example. With budget cuts and accelerated change and uncertainty, leaders are constantly pressured into rethinking the way they deliver services to the public. The public needs government agencies to reinvent their service delivery model—to be more efficient and effective. Hacking away with time-honored practices isn't going to cut it anymore.

For SMEs, renewal powers growth and competitive advantage. As I explain in my book, *Performance Management for Agile Organizations*, agility is the new measure for business success.[2] And a trusting environment is a critical ingredient of an agile enterprise.

Notwithstanding its importance, studies show levels of trust at all-time lows.[3] Considering the scale of layoffs across most industries during the GFC, declining trust levels among employees is understandable. The question leaders ought to be grappling with in the post-GFC environment is: How can trust levels be rebuilt in a jaded workplace?

A culture of trust starts at the top, like any organization culture. Nothing erodes trust faster than managers not walking the talk. If there's chronic distrust of the senior team, then it permeates the length and breadth of the enterprise. To build, rebuild, or sustain trust, leaders must set the tone. Demonstrating genuine interest in the welfare of people, believing in their competence and reliability, and communicating openly and honestly are the cornerstones of establishing a trusting work relationship.

I now want to return to the four key elements leaders need to be mindful of.

People naturally want to be treated fairly in comparison with others. Fair treatment leads to a feeling of psychological safety. Three types of fairness are relevant here. One form of fairness is the equal distribution of resources. For example, if an employee benefits from being given access to more modern equipment over another employee in a similar position, this will be viewed as unfair by at least one person. Apart from the person missing out on the new equipment, others observing this inequality may also see this as an unfair advantage. Faith and trust in the manager allocating these resources will inevitably be eroded, consequently.

A second form of fairness is procedural fairness. Procedural fairness refers to how work systems and processes are used. If one person must jump through all the hoops, and another person gets a free ride in similar circumstances, this is likely to be considered unfair—at least in the eyes of the disadvantaged person, for example. Equal access to the organization's systems and processes is the basis of procedural fairness.

A third source of fairness is interactional fairness. Interactional fairness is about the way people are treated in their deliberations with others. Take, for example, a manager who—intentionally or otherwise—ignores the thoughts and ideas of a colleague on several occasions. And simultaneously, this manager pays excessive attention to another person's point-of-view in a meeting. The person being overlooked may think this is unfair. Everyone else observing this behavior—may consider this unfair too.

Fairness counts—whether it's distribution fairness, procedural fairness, or interaction fairness. It counts. It can boost or erode trust between people at work.

Apart from the manager's treatment of people they work with, the second trust builder (or destroyer) is recognizing people's efforts at work. The way it's done, or not done, can have a positive or negative impact. Employees generally want to be recognized for doing a good job. According to a recent study, recognition is the key to harvesting employee engagement.[4] People who don't feel appreciated at work are more likely to leave—or at least want to leave—their job to work elsewhere. Based on a large study of employees in the United States, extending over a decade, Adrian Gostick and Chester Elton report some disheartening statistics:

- 79 per cent of employees who quit their jobs cite a lack of appreciation as a key reason for leaving.
- 65 per cent of North Americans report that they didn't receive any recognition in the previous year.[5]

These figures are even more glaring when it's estimated that employee turnover costs the US economy $11 Billion a year.[6]

Recognizing employees—done fairly and in concert with fostering their human spirit at work—builds engagement and trust. And the best and most authentic way of doing this—despite all the fanfare of public recognition—is in private, one-on-one.

The third approach to building trust is giving people a clear direction. Setting clear, challenging, but attainable goals—not vague, impossible, and out-of-reach goals—is a trust and confidence builder. Most people want to make a worthy contribution at work. People should be stretched to meet higher standards at work. Capable leaders do this by setting well-defined and inspiring goals. A very important, yet often neglected role of leadership is to persistently and consistently communicate the goals of the enterprise. This delivers the three Cs—certainty, clarity, and confidence.

Actively supporting the development needs of people is the fourth approach to create trust. People are typically interested in their own growth and development, both as an employee and a person. Training and development opportunities can expand knowledge, build skill, and renew confidence. The prosperity of all enterprises is dependent upon the growth of the people working in it. In other words, if employees aren't growing, then the organization isn't growing. Learning that has relevance and meaning is undoubtedly a motivational force for the people undertaking it.

People strive to meet their full potential through the developmental opportunities they take on. We discussed the concept of *mastery* in Chap. 2, as intrinsically motivating for the knowledge worker. Giving people the opportunity for personal mastery shows them that they are valued and builds trust.

People are the heart and soul of any enterprise. Without engaged and committed employees, there's no business. Trust is a reciprocal arrangement. Once trust is lost—as you've no doubt experienced—it's extremely hard to resuscitate it.

Pillar 4: Show Genuine Appreciation

As I've illustrated in Chap. 4, surveys consistently indicate that employees don't receive enough—or any—appreciation for the work they do. It's a significant reason why capable people ultimately leave to work elsewhere. But leaders nevertheless find it difficult or unimportant to show appreciation at work. It's baffling. Showing appreciation doesn't cost a cent. It's quick and pleasant to do.

In Chap. 13, we'll cover the encouraging conversation in much more detail. But showing appreciation is also part of being an authentic leader; it's the first step to encouragement.

> **Where the Rubber Meets the Road…**
>
> **Thanks for Coming to Work Today**
>
> A senior executive I coach told me an interesting story. She said she sometimes thank people for coming to work when they arrive first thing in the morning. "Thanks for coming to work today," she'd say to the startled employees as they arrive in the morning and plunk themselves down in front of their computer screen with their first coffee for the day. Gathering herself, this employee looked up at her boss—eyes wide open—and asked, "Did I have a choice?" With a confident smile, good eye contact, and not missing a beat, this leader responded, "Yes, you did have a choice, as a matter of fact. You always have a choice." That employee may not have considered—coming to work as a choice, but yes, she did in fact have a choice about coming to work that day. This leader was simply showing her appreciation in a thought-provoking way.

Paul White, psychologist and author, in his recent article, *Appreciation at Work: Two Major Misconceptions Leaders Hold*, highlight two fallacies about appreciation in the workplace.[7] He says that one misconception is that the purpose of showing appreciation is to make people feel good about themselves at work. It's a delusion because you can't make people feel good; they're the ones who make that decision. The leader can't do this. They can cheer people up. But it's only a temporary state. The other person soon re-adjusts their attitude back to the way they decide to feel. So, this isn't necessarily a valid—or effective—reason for showing appreciation at work.

The other misconception is that by showing appreciation, productivity inevitably improves. Productivity won't increase, however, if it isn't genuine appreciation. Put another way: If the only reason a leader expresses appreciation is to boost output, it won't work. But that's not to say that there isn't a connection between genuine recognition and performance.

Showing appreciation for authentic reasons—not with an ulterior motive to manipulate performance—is undoubtedly good for business. White suggests the following benefits:

- increased daily attendance;
- decreased tardiness;
- faithful adherence to following policies and procedures;
- reduced conflict in the office;
- increased productivity; and
- more satisfied customers.[8]

These benefits can either directly or indirectly positively impact performance with sincere gratitude.

Let's explore this misconception that by showing appreciation, you routinely increase productivity. If the primary purpose of appreciation is financial gain, it doesn't work. People see through this façade. Appreciation to boost performance is an act of manipulation of the very people it's targeted at. There's a hidden agenda. It's not authentic. It's therefore a selfish and manipulative exercise. That's the reason it fails to improve employee performance.

Instead of higher productivity, cynicism and resentment ensue. People begrudge the idea that they are being deployed to achieve greater productivity by a systemic program of recognition. This isn't honest appreciation. That's why it doesn't work. Appreciation ought to be authentic.

What's the true purpose of communicating appreciation, then? Really, showing appreciation should be about conveying respect and recognizing a person's value. The potential positives in performance outputs ought to be a secondary consideration. I understand the fine line. But the key point here is that the leader shouldn't be praising a person because they want improved productivity.

What's more, appreciation doesn't always have to be about the work someone does. A leader can genuinely appreciate the innate skills, talents, and capabilities a person possesses. The appreciation could, for instance, be passed on for a thoughtful insight or positive comment. It doesn't have to be for 'good work.'

Outstanding leaders understand that people have inherent value beyond the work obligations contained within their job description. If we restrict appreciation to a key performance indicator (KPI), it dehumanizes the act of appreciation. In other words, it's only the work that people do that's appreciated, not the people themselves. The more impressionable the appreciation, the more likely it's going to be about the person, rather than their work. We still need to acknowledge the good work people do in their jobs. But appreciation can go beyond work successes.

If we take a moment and observe, most people can be appreciated for who they are as people. Some people, for example, have a sunny disposition that lights up a room. Others have the capability of breaking things down into bit size pieces. Whatever it is, a leader should recognize and show appreciation for these innate talents too (see strengths and talent conversation, Chap. 20).

Delve a little deeper into the lives of people outside the front gate of the organization, and you open the opportunity of appreciating some things about the *employee* as a *human being*. There's probably some things you mightn't appreciate too!

But in terms of appreciation, consider, for example, the quiet admin officer you pass each morning in the corridor might be a single parent and coping with these pressures gracefully. Or, the gregarious salesperson in the office may devote their spare time and energy to a worthy local cause in their local community. Or, the older, less mobile customer support officer you see every morning may have achieved great things on the sporting field in their day, and so on. Taking an interest in people's lives beyond the job they do. This can unearth many interesting insights worthy of your praise.

Showing appreciation isn't necessarily about making people feel good. And it isn't a way of extracting more effort from them in their job. As Paul White puts it,

> The foundation of authentic appreciation is respecting and valuing employees for who they are as people, in addition to the contributions they make to the organization.[9]

Pillar 5: Build for the Future

Challenging unhelpful behavior—the second task-focused pillar we discussed in Chap. 5—and build for the future are connected. The purpose of any constructive conversation is to build for the future; that is, changing the poor behavior of the past to be improved behavior in the future. Challenging unhelpful behavior—as we've discussed—should be based on one or more critical incidents observed in the past. But challenging that behavior is eventually about building for a better future.

Despite what it may appear on the surface, challenging unhelpful behavior is as much about planning for the future, as it is about learning from the past. By drawing attention to past incidents, the leader's focus should be on supporting the team member to rectify this for the future. What needs to change? How can the person be supported to make those changes? are the questions the leader ought to ultimately focus on. An essential pillar of the authentic conversation is then to prepare for the future.

Building for the future is looking ahead. Looking ahead means planning. The focus here is on the person. Constructive conversations are about agreeing on making changes for the future, not dwelling in the past. Critical incidents are used to exemplify the changes needed. But a leader needs to strike the right balance between discussing past indiscretions and future aspirations.

I've always adhered to the philosophy that we should live in the moment, learn from the past, and plan for the future—although I must admit, I don't always practice it! We can't change the past; however, we can learn from it. The leader's attention in these conversations should center on the question: *What are the important lessons we can pick up from the past?*

It means that finger pointing, blame, and doling out guilt have no place in authentic conversations or indeed, the authentic workplace. Build for the future is essentially about exploring what needs to be done tomorrow, and beyond. What needs to change? Planning for the future is a collaborative exercise. It should to be discussed cooperatively between leader and team member for an optimum outcome. And the day-to-day focus of the leader and everyone else, ought to be in the here and now. This is the most constructive way to live and work, as challenging as it can be sometimes.

All useful conversations are eventually about some type of forward projection. Even awkward conversations about resolving misunderstandings in the past are in the end about moving forward, hopefully, with a more complete understanding and extra empathy. Whenever two people have a difference-of-opinion, the aim of dialog is two-fold. First, to understand the other person's point-of-view. And second, to manage the differences for the future.

Build for the future is a pillar of the authentic conversation because it's essentially about doing something constructive because of the conversation. People can and do control their futures to a certain extent. Discussing the future is a genuine attempt to improve things moving forward.

All 10 conversations I cover in Parts II and III consider the future. Take the climate review conversation (Chap. 19), for example. The main thrust of the climate review conversation is to discuss a team member's job satisfaction, their observations of morale within the immediate team, and reflections on the quality of communication within and outside the team. More specifically, after the leader invites the team member to rate their current job satisfaction on a scale of 1 to 10 (10 being high and 1 being low), the follow up question is: *Why did you rate it as such?* The conversation then moves to how the rating (job satisfaction) might be improved in the future. What could the leader do, if anything, to assist the team member to increase their level of job satisfaction (beyond extra pay!)? What needs to change? What can be done differently? How can we progress? And so forth. Without a future orientation, the conversation isn't going to be productive.

The leader builds for the future with good questions. Questions such as, *What needs to change?* Or, *Can I get your commitment in the future to do this (or not do that)?* Or, *How will you approach this situation next time?* Or, *Are you open to trying something new next time?* The authenticity in building for the future is based on the practical necessity to do and think differently.

A developmental or performance conversation without some commitment to change isn't productive—it's a talk-fest. Otherwise people are left hanging, without a constructive path to change. It's principally the leader's job to steer the conversation in the direction of the future. The eventual emphasis should be on what's going to be different.

Building for the future can be about both the leader and team member. From the leader's point-of-view, they should look within and ask themselves: *What have I gained from this conversation? And how will that change things for the future?* In sum, it means: *What have I learnt from this conversation?* It's not always an action that requires change. It could be the way the leader thinks, or perceives a situation or person. It's like looking in the mirror.

So, it's not always just about the other person in the conversation. Some honest leadership self-reflection is also authentic. Sometimes this can be the most challenging part of building for the future. We don't always like what we see in the mirror and can dismiss it by looking away. The other person in the dialog needs clarity and commitment about what to think or do in the future. Whether it happens is a separate issue. But a conversation that finishes with building for the future is a constructive place to end the dialog. Some candid consideration about the leader's role is part of this process.

This brings us to the end of Chap. 6 and Part I. As I pointed out, the five pillars of authentic conversation are not necessarily conversations per se. Although some of the 10 conversations you'll be exposed to shortly—and hopefully use—are based on some of these pillars. But the more important takeout is that the five pillars are characteristics of authentic conversation in general. Each pillar has its place in authentic workplace conversations.

To recap: Agreeing on expectations (Pillar 1) nurtures mutual understanding and lessens uncertainty. Challenging unhelpful behavior (Pillar 2) is concerned with upholding and continuing acceptable workplace practices. Establish a trusting relationship is the foundation for all productive conversations (Pillar 3). Productive conversations build trust. But leaders ought to strive to develop and sustain trust in all they say and do. Showing genuine appreciation (Pillar 4) is about respecting the employee as a human being. And build for the future (Pillar 5) is based on using the conversation as a tool of change. You would do well to keep these five pillars top-of-mind in all your interactions with others.

In Part II, we consider the types of conversations available for leaders that are people-focused—conversations that develop the individual. We begin with the coaching conversation.

The Top 10 Key Points …

1. In this final chapter of Part I, we reviewed the three other people-focused pillars of the authentic conversations framework: Establish a trusting relationship, Show genuine appreciation, and Challenge unhelpful behavior.
2. Trust and authenticity are related. Authentic communicating builds trust.
3. Trust is also a precondition for innovation and continuous improvement.
4. A culture of trust—or any culture—starts at the top.
5. Treating people fairly is a good starting point for showing genuine appreciation.
6. Surveys consistently indicate that employees don't receive enough—or any—appreciation for the work they do.
7. Showing appreciation should be about conveying respect and recognizing a person's value.
8. Building for the future is about looking ahead. Looking ahead means planning.
9. Build for the future is a pillar of the authentic conversation because it's essentially about doing something constructive in the future.
10. A conversation without some commitment to the future isn't productive—it's a talk-fest.

Notes

1. McManus, J. & Mosca, J. (2015). "Strategies to build trust and improve employee engagement." *International Journal of Management and Information Systems*, 19, 1, 37–42.
2. Baker, T.B. (2016). Performance management for agile organizations: Overthrowing the eight management myths that hold businesses back. London: Palgrave Macmillan.
3. CIPD (2012). *Where has all the trust gone?* London, Chartered Institute of Personnel and Development retrieved from http://www.trustinorganizations.com/Resources/Documents/WhereHasAllTheTrustGone.pdf.pdf.
4. http://www.naylornetwork.com/ahh-nwl/articles/index-v2.asp?aid=141503&issueID=22503.
5. Russell, J.E.A (2010). "Career coach: Recognition not only boosts employees, but can also give a lift to the bottom line." *The Washington Post*. Retrieved at http://www.washingtonpost.com/wp-dyn/content/article/2010/10/22/AR2010102205919.html.

6. Lipman, V. (2012). "Study explores drivers of employee engagement." *Forbes*. Retrieved from http://www.forbes.com/sites/victorlipman/2012/12/14/study-explores-drivers-of-employee-engagement/#670a238977bc.
7. White, P. (2015). Appreciation at work: Two major misconceptions leaders hold. Retrieved at https://www.entrepreneur.com/article/244657.
8. Ibid.
9. Ibid.

Part II

Five Developmental Conversations

7

Conversation 1: The Coaching Conversation

The best coaching conversations can be described as journeys of discovery.

Georgiou bounds into Catherine's office unannounced and stressed. His face is as white as a ghost. Georgiou is seeking some advice from Catherine, his boss. Catherine adopts an open-door policy and encouraged her staff to 'drop in' when they needed too. This was one such occasion.

"What's wrong, Georgiou? You look troubled." "I am," he replied, plunking himself on the leather sofa. "I can't seem to get Julie to stop being negative around the office," he says, getting up to close the door to Catherine's office. "I see."

"Tell me what the ideal situation would look like." "Well, I want zero negativity from her. Now, all I get is a barrage of negative comments and complaints about everyone and everything."

"So, what's the current situation? What's getting in the way of zero negativity?" "Julie just can't help herself. Whether it's in meetings or in the office, it's just blame, blame, blame!" replied an obviously agitated Georgiou.

"What have you tried to do to stop this?" "I have given her a pep talk and explained the consequences on morale by being negative." "Is it working?" "No, it's not helping." "What else could you try then?" "I suppose I could talk to her about why she feels the need to express this negativity."

"What else can you try, Georgiou?" probed Catherine. "I suppose I could set a target with her and get her agreement. Like, for example, to try to not express a negative word for a day in the office." "What if she is successful, what then?" Catherine chimed in. "I could let her know that I noticed and am pleased she's trying."

"Which of those options do you think might be worth a go, Georgiou?" "I think I'll try and sit down with Julie and set a target to spend a day in the office without any negativity. And at the end of the day, I'll sit down with her and debrief. This might be a step in the right direction."

"Okay, that sounds like a plan. Do you need me to help in some way?" "No, you have been helpful just listening to me and coaching me through a process."

Georgiou walked out of Catherine's office with more energy than when he came in a few minutes earlier.

The number of people-centered conversations we can engage in at work is limitless. In Part I, we navigated the terrain for cultivating an authentic workplace. Conversations are the essential vehicle for realizing authenticity at work. In Part II, I'm going to cover five developmental conversations leaders should be regularly having with team members. Each of these five conversation types have their place. The conversations I discuss in this part are supported with an application tool. One type of conversation isn't more important than another. They all have their place. However, you'll find some easier than others. Engaging in developmental dialog is the hallmark of a people-centered leader. Done frequently enough, with sincerity, and some capability, promotes dignity at work.

You'll be familiar with many of these types of developmental conversations I'm about to share. Being familiar with something doesn't mean it's being practiced though! We'll look at some of the barriers to conducting these conversations. Moreover, I'll identify the key principles for success. I'll also join the dots between these conversations for a more productive, harmonious, and authentic place of work. We'll consider too, how these people-focused conversations foster human spirit and work—the concept we discussed in Chap. 2. Wherever possible, I'll make the connection between the five pillars we covered in the last two chapters and these developmental conversations to illustrate authentic communication.

And speaking of application, some of these developmental conversations will feel more comfortable for you to initiate than others. Perhaps there's one or two types of conversation you've avoided? That's okay. But I want to encourage you to try them all; I want you to put them into your leadership toolkit. Just as a carpenter needs a full set of tools to deal with all the building projects they confront, so too the leader needs the full array of tools. Each kind of conversation has a place in the leader's arsenal.

Even if you're a 'believer' and engage in thousands of conversations, getting better at them should be your goal. There's always room for improvement. I hope to enlighten you—perhaps just a little—on your leadership journey.

Apart from having the right frame-of-mind, there are three characteristics that determine the success of any conversation. One characteristic is your skills-set and preparedness to have the conversation. Another factor is the other person's skills-set and their level of readiness for the conversation. Yet another aspect is the context or situation you are facing at the time of conversing. The three characteristics all blend in like the ingredients of a cake.

By improving your skills-set, you will positively impact the other two variables. Working on conversation capabilities also can change your attitude about yourself, the people you lead, and leadership itself. These two factors can also alter the attitude of the person you are conversing with.

Improving your capacity to have more productive conversations can certainly influence the people you work with and the situations you face. You can influence the attitude of the team member with conversation skills; for example, by listening actively, the other person may become more engaged in the conversation. Or, being more mindful of the surrounding circumstances of the conversation helps too. For example, knowing that someone is making a genuine effort to change means you can be encouraging—as well as firm—when discussing their need for improvement. Getting better at conversations skills greatly improves your ability to be effective.

In this chapter, we tackle the coaching conversation. It may appear strange to you that I'm linking the two words: *coaching* and *conversation*. Is coaching really a conversation? Effective coaching is just that—a conversation between a coach and coachee. Good coaching is a dialog between two or more people.

Traditionally, we think of coaching as teaching—the master, with their superior skills and knowledge, teaches the apprentice a skill, or imparts knowledge on a subject-matter. But to be more influential, the coach needs to engross the coachee in the learning experience. This is accomplished by doing more listening and less teaching. Good coaches ask lots of questions to involve the other person in the learning experience. For this reason alone, coaching is a type of developmental conversation. The best coaches are catalysts who positively change people's thinking patterns, as well as their future actions. Shifting people's perspectives comes through engagement. And engagement happens with genuine dialog and authentic conversation. When people are fully immersed in a learning experience via a coaching conversation, they tend to be more receptive to alternative ways of thinking.

Tony Grant and Jane Greene in their book, *Solution Focused Coaching: Managing People in a Complex World* say this about coaching:

> Coaching is about creating positive directed change. It is about helping people to develop their potential. Managers can use coaching to enhance and increase the performance of individuals and teams.

They describe coaching as a

> collaborative, solution-focused, result-orientated and systematic process in which the coach facilitates the enhancement of work performance, life experience, self-directed learning and personal growth of individuals.[1]

The coaching conversation guides—rather than informs—the coachee. The best coaching conversation can be described as a journey of discovery. Coaching should be much more than communicating a prescriptive set of instructions for an employee to follow. A collaborative coaching approach requires more discipline and patience. We know it takes less effort to instruct someone what to do, than help them discover what to do themselves. It's not only easier; it's quicker.

But it's less effective. And in the long run consider this: It can be more time-consuming, not to mention frustrating, when the other person doesn't 'get it'. The telling approach—being less effective—means repetitious 'coaching' sessions, not to mention the frustration that comes with that.

The right coaching conversation can ignite a person's intrinsic motivation. By collaborating instead of prescribing, the leader respects the independence of the individual and their growth. The coachee ultimately decides what course-of-action to take. This taps into the dimensions of autonomy and mastery I spoke of in Chap. 2. The main purpose of the coaching conversation is to build capability, and this is consistent with Dan Pink's concept of mastery. Mastery is typically achieved when the coachee has the autonomy in exercising their learning options. A good coaching conversation can also help to affirm direction and purpose—the third dimension of intrinsic motivation. Coaching conversations—done the right way—can help to cultivate one's human spirit in the work they're doing.

Good coaching conversations cover all five pillars we covered in Chaps. 5 and 6. When a leader devotes time to coaching someone, it signals trust in the coachee. You wouldn't bother spending time coaching someone, if you didn't ultimately believe they could achieve success, would you? During the coaching conversation, expectations are explained. This builds confidence and trust too. Further, coaching conversations offer the leader an opportunity to express their appreciation of coachee and challenge any unhelpful behavior. Coaching is about the future. The purpose of the coaching conversation is preparation to tackle something sooner or later. All the authenticity pillars can be part of the coaching conversation.

Corridor Coaching

In our book, *Conversations at Work* (co-authored with Aubrey Warren), we talk about the power of 'corridor coaching.'[2] Coaching is characteristically thought of as an event, scheduled ahead of time; the coaching session is structured and planned. Time is set aside. In many cases this is true. But think of coaching also as a spontaneous process that can occur at any time, in any place, with anyone. Developmental coaching conversations can take place informally, impulsively, and briefly. We might call it *corridor coaching*.

An observant leader is alert to opportunities to have a coaching conversation. As the name suggests, the corridor conversation can occur on the spur-of-the-moment, with no warning or planning. Being attentive and mindful are the only requirements of the leader on these unplanned occasions.

For example, Juliette 'bumps into' Jamie, one of his team members, in the corridor. She takes the opportunity to ask Jamie how he went with the firm's new client. Juliette starts by congratulating Jamie on winning the new business and asks him what the biggest lesson he learnt from the sales experience. Jamie thinks for a moment before stating that he thought that following up his proposal made the difference. Juliette asks Jamie how they intend to apply that insight in future. Jamie points out that it affirmed his view of the value of following up proposals and intends to make this a habit. That's a spontaneous, quick, but effective coaching conversation.

> **Where the Rubber Meets the Road …**
>
> **Impromptu Meeting in the Hallway**
>
> Iqbal and Joe cross paths in the hallway. Iqbal is Joe's manager. Joe has just tailored a successful solution for a satisfied customer. Specifically, he's carried out a safety audit for a customer and unearthed several areas for business improvement—this resulted in a safer and more productive work-setting for his customer.
>
> Iqbal stops and says, "Hi Joe. Congratulations on completing that safety audit with the new client. I hear it was a great success." "Thanks Iqbal. The client was very happy with the outcome." "That's great! Well done."
>
> "What was the one big lesson you learn from that project, Joe?" Iqbal inquires. "Well, I learnt not to make assumptions; to check my facts first up. I guess I learnt to keep an open-mind. And probably, the most important lesson was to focus on the solution." "Great to hear," replied Iqbal with enthusiasm.
>
> "How will that knowledge help you in the future?" "I guess I need to go into workplaces with an open-mind and not make assumptions until I have all the facts. It made me more aware of the need to find practical solutions to problems the client is facing."
>
> "That's great learning, Joe. Keep up the good work. See you later. I am off to a meeting." "Thanks, Iqbal."
>
> That's a corridor coaching conversation.

Here's another example of coaching-on-the-spot. Mary has come to speak to her manager Patricia. Patricia isn't expecting to see Patricia. Patricia indicates that she has a problem with two of her team members who are at war with each other. She doesn't know how to deal with this. Patricia politely stops Mary from 'downloading' her frustrations. Here is how the conversation unfolds:

"Mary, what's the ideal outcome you're looking for?" "Well, I want these two people to work harmoniously as part of my team," replies Mary with a tone of frustration.

"What's getting in the way of that, then?" Patricia asks. "Two of my colleagues had an altercation the other day and both blamed each other for not getting something done. There was a miscommunication and they both think the other is at fault."

"Okay, so apart from that incident, they've been working well together, have they?" Patricia asks, seeking clarification. "Pretty much." "So, the issue is the incident?" "Yes, that's right. I don't know what to do about it."

"Okay then, what are your options, Mary?" "I don't know," says Mary, with a sigh of resignation. "That's why I thought I would come and see you." "Well, what do you think you can do to resolve this?"

"I've thought about sitting them down separately and having a conversation with them to get to the bottom of it." "Okay, what else can you do?" "I've thought that perhaps the best way of managing this is to call a meeting with the two of them and trying to resolve this together." "Okay, what else?" "I've thought about getting the whole team together and explaining the importance of team work and the need to have everyone working together."

"Okay, which of those three options do you think may work best, Mary?" Patricia concludes.

"I think I probably should sit down and have a conversation with each of them first to get to the bottom of the conflict and then perhaps bring them together and collaborate on a possible solution." "Sounds like a good plan to me," affirms Patricia.

"What can I do to help?" "You've already been helpful talking this through with me, Patricia," "Great!" "Well, give it a go and come back and let me know what happens." "Thanks, Patricia."

You may be thinking: *That looks easy, but surely, it's got to be more difficult in real life*. It's that easy, if you're disciplined enough to listen and ask good questions that encourage the other person to think and talk. The key is *not* to jump in and solve the problem for the other person. That's probably the hardest part—not giving the coachee the benefit of your wisdom. By asking open-ended questions, you're coaching the other person to come to the right conclusions themselves. It respects their independence to make decisions.

The conversation between Patricia and Mary follows a great coaching process called GROW. You would do well to adopt it in these inevitable unprompted corridor conversations—although this model can be used in any coaching situation, spontaneous or otherwise. I explain this model in the next chapter.

The Top 10 Key Points …

1. Improving your capacity to have more productive conversations can certainly influence the people you work with and the situations you face.
2. There are three factors that determine the success of any conversation.
3. One factor is your skills-set and readiness to have the conversation.
4. Another variable is the other person's skills-set and their level of preparedness for the conversation.
5. Yet another factor is the context or situation you are facing at the time of conversing.
6. Effective coaching is a conversation between a coach and coachee. Good coaching is a dialog between two or more people.
7. The best coaches are catalysts for positively change people's thinking, as well as their actions. Shifting people's perspectives comes through engagement with people and the environment.
8. The right coaching conversation can ignite a person's intrinsic motivation. By collaborating instead of prescribing, the leader respects the independence of the individual and their growth.
9. Coaching conversations can take place informally, spontaneously, and briefly. We might call it corridor coaching.
10. By asking open-ended questions, you're coaching the other person to come to the right conclusions themselves.

Notes

1. Greene, J. and Grant, A.M. (2003). Solution-focused coaching: Managing people in a complex world. Harlow: Pearson.
2. Baker, T. & Warren, A. (2015). Conversations at work: Promoting a culture of conversation in a changing workplace. London: Palgrave Macmillan.

8

Using GROW for a Better Coaching Conversation

Managers ought to remind themselves that they're not in the business of answering questions; they are, more in effect, in the business of asking questions.

In this chapter, I explain the GROW model in detail and how it can be applied to conduct a positive coaching conversation.

While no one person can be clearly identified as the originator of *GROW*, Graham Alexander, Alan Fine, and Sir John Whitmore all made significant contributions to developing the model.[1] GROW stands for *Goal, Reality, Options*, and *What next?* Let's break it down, step-by-step.

Goal

The intention in the first stage of GROW is to set a goal. This is so the coachee can walk away from the coaching conversation with a tangible objective. And as leader, you are clear what they're wanting to achieve.

When someone comes to you with an issue, problem, or challenge and wants to *dump* on you, politely stop them and ask them this question: *What is the ideal outcome you are trying to achieve?* This forces the other person to articulate to you what success looks like. If the other person can't explain what the ideal result ought to be, it means they haven't thought it through.

What's more, if the coachee doesn't know what the ideal outcome is, then it's impossible for them to know where to start. Ask the coachee upfront to consider the result they are aiming for. As the coach, you should attempt to establish this outcome first up. The coachee may not be able to articulate a specific goal at the beginning of the conversation. Persevere. The use of further questioning and probing enables the other person to formulate a well-defined and realistic goal.

Here are some questions that might assist clarifying the *goal*:

- *For you to be satisfied in this situation, what would it look like?*
- *What are you trying to achieve?*
- *How will you know you've been successful?*
- *What are you aiming for?*

Reality

Once they've explained what the goal is, you can then ask a different question: *What is getting in the way?* or *What is stopping you getting to this result?* This question guides the coachee to specify the core problem or challenge that's getting in the way of them achieving the goal. Asking about the roadblocks after identifying the goal means that they are encouraged to consider only those things that are barriers to achieving the goal. Other matters peripheral to the situation need not be discussed. So, with as few as two questions, both of you in the coaching conversation have identified a goal and the main obstacle in the way of achieving success.

As I'm sure you know, too much time can be consumed by the team member giving a long-winded explanation of the circumstances blocking them from fixing the problem. Other less relevant or irrelevant matters are often raised at the beginning of the conversation. This wastes valuable time. You've no doubt been told in training courses that leaders are supposed to listen to team members without interrupting; to be patient, in other words.

That's partially true of course. But by being patient and not interrupting the coachee when they are grappling with a problem can be time-consuming and unconstructive. Often the employee wants to get things off their chest. A more constructive approach when this occurs is to narrow down the discussion to the real barriers in the way. All the other stuff is incidental and needless. What are the things getting in the way? is the focus at this stage of the coaching conversation.

The options for finding a solution become clearer after covering the current situation. The intention here is to assist the coachee to clarify the main barriers. By peeling away the layers of the onion, you get to the core. Asking the right questions helps the coachee recognize the reality of their situation.

Here are some questions that might assist to understand the *reality*:

- *What are the key things getting in the way of you achieving this goal or outcome?*
- *What are the barriers to success?*
- *What's stopping you?*
- *Can you identify the obstacles?*

Options

Once the coachee has satisfactorily described their reality, and the barriers, your role is to enable them to generate some options to break these roadblocks.

You might find the next question challenging to ask: *What options are open for you to resolving this?* It is a hard question because you—no doubt familiar with the options available—are probably tempted to offer a ready-made solution to the problem. The *answer* is most likely on the tip of your tongue.

But contributing a solution—no matter how well intended and workable it is—isn't helpful. Why? You want the other person to *own* the solution, to be emotionally committed to resolving the problem. Giving the coachee the answer is not the answer.

Notice the question: *What options are open for you to resolving this?* contains the word *options*, not option. It suggests there's more than one option. By asking for options—instead of one option—you open the possibility of unearthing several possibilities. A good supplementary question to ask is, *What other options could you consider?* Be patient and wait for the other person to offer other alternatives. Don't judge. Don't evaluate. Just listen and ask for more options.

Let's recap. At this stage, you both know what the ideal outcome is (goal), what's stopping the coachee from achieving this outcome (reality), and several options for resolving the dilemma (options). Good progress so far.

In most of my coaching conversations using GROW, I've been astonished at the inherent capability of people to see their way through issues, resolve problems, and identify development needs. In most cases, it's not necessary for me to intrude overtly into the natural process of self-discovery.

In the *Options* phase—like the other phases of GROW—the best strategy is to ask open-ended questions. Successful coaching conversations don't always have to draw out particularly novel ideas. Often, they bring previous thoughts into sharper focus and help the coachee decide whether certain choices are doable.

At this stage of the coaching conversation, it's possible the coachee will ask for your advice. They're naturally interested in your perspective as leader. Also, the coachee—with a conventional view of coaching—will think it's the leader's job to give them assistance—to hold their hand. This typical expectation isn't a license to you to start giving advice, however, as tempting as it surely is.

Nevertheless, the coachee may feel blocked—they're stumped for answers. Or, they may advance some unrealistic options. Or, the coachee may be covering old ground. What then does the coach do?

In these situations, the leader's job isn't to rescue the coachee. It's the team member's responsibility to do the heavy lifting. The coaching conversation is about enabling the coachee to find the way forward. It's about giving them the freedom and autonomy to make their own choices and decisions. This is done by asking more questions, seeking clarification, and *not* answering the coachee's questions.

Sooner or later—with patience and applying what you've learnt—the coachee should have several viable options available for consideration. These possibilities have come, preferably, from the coachee's insight, experience, or creativity. The coach can add some possible additional options, but only after the coachee has hit the wall—not before.

Here are some questions that might assist with generating *options*:

- *What have you thought about doing to resolve this?*
- *What are your options?*
- *Who can help you resolve this?*
- *What are some other possibilities?*

What Next?

And the 'W' in GROW stands for *What next?* In other words, at this stage you invite the coachee to consider their options and select the best possibility. Or, in the case of the example of Mary and Patricia in the previous chapter, choose a combination of options. Reassure your colleague that you will support them in their plan-of-action. Affirm that the coachee is on the right track (assuming they are) and then promise to take an interest in their progress and development.

At this stage of the coaching conversation, you've arrived at the action phase—where the rubber meets the road. A successful coaching conversation concludes with a well-defined and feasible course-of-action. You should discuss with the coachee their reasons for choosing the plan. Talking over the rationale for the next step assesses the coachee's line-of-thinking. This final part of the conversation gauges the coachee's level of certainty and confidence in putting their choice into action. By doing this, it is likely to be reassuring for both you and the coachee.

The person you are coaching will hopefully have more than one option on the table. So, the aim at this stage is to narrow the possibilities down to a workable plan. Through the GROW process, the coachee arrives at a final course-of-action, broken down into specific steps. This is the moment to challenge the coachee to assess the implications of their chosen action. Is it practical? What are the possible obstacles? And what support will be required from you and others?

What next? is the time to drill down to details. This involves tangible actions and necessary steps, when they will be taken, who ought to be involved, and how success will be evaluated.

Here are some questions that might assist with considering *what next?*

- Which of these options is the most feasible?
- Why have you chosen this course-of-action?
- What's the next step?
- What support will you need from me and others?

The Rationale for Using GROW

GROW offers a simple, practical, and comprehensive framework for leaders to facilitate productive coaching conversations. It's a great method for guiding a discussion with a team member who is fully engaged in the conversation. It doesn't require unattainable skill, training in psychology, or a background in psychotherapy.

Two assumptions support GROW. First, that the person being coached is fully functional, not dysfunctional; they can take responsibility for their working life. The second assumption is that coaching is most effective when working in partnership. These two assumptions are compatible with the concepts of human spirit and work and workplace dignity we covered in Part I.

As I said in the previous chapter, there's a common misconception that coaching is about a leader imparting their knowledge, wisdom, and experience on the apprentice. I think managers—when buttonholed by team members—tend to spoon-feed them answers for two compelling reasons. First, the manager—being human—craves the feeling of being needed. By being the source of vital information, the manager feels valued and appreciated. It's a quick sugar hit.

But managers ought to remind themselves that they're not in the business of answering questions; they are, more in effect, in the business of asking questions. To paraphrase that familiar proverb,

> give a man a fish and you feed him for a day; teach a man to fish and you feed him for a lifetime.[2]

The coaching conversation is all about *enabling* the other person to achieve sustainable success. This is achieved by asking, instead of, answering questions.

The second reason the manager finds it seductive to give an answer to a team member's question is simply that it's quick. The manager probably thinks it'll take too much unnecessary time to do otherwise. After all, *Why not just give them the answer and move on?* is the usual thought process. But, it'll eventually take more time servicing people with a speedy response. How so? By giving a colleague the answer, the manager is training them to be totally dependent on them. It's simpler for the team member to come back again for an answer from the boss than think for themselves.

What's more, it creates the false impression that the manager has *all* the answers. With this belief, the team member will perpetually go to their manager for answers on a wide range of matters, particularly when the manager gets a feeling of being needed. It's convenient for the team member; much more convenient than stretching their brain by thinking for themselves! Briefly, it trains people to be reliant on the boss, not self-reliant (learning to catch the fish). And as I said, the manager rationalizes that giving an answer saves valuable time. But what the answer-giving manager forgets—in their haste to impart their wisdom and experience— is that they're training the other person to incessantly interrupt them on trivial matters.

The know-it-all manager may reason that they'll be wasting their time using the GROW model. Spending valuable minutes listening to a long-winded explanation from the team member about the circumstances surrounding a problem can, after all, be perceived as unnecessary painful. But the GROW format reduces—not increases—the time taken and teaches the employee to be self-sufficient. And being self-sufficient translates to less frivolous interruptions for the manager. It saves time in the long run.

Another advantage of using GROW is that it's ideally suited to the work-setting. It's problem-based and prompts the leader and team member to discuss a range of issues affecting the work challenge. The leader's role should be to guide the discussion and assist team members to think about the solution at a deeper level—than would otherwise be the case—by giving a quick response.

Managers by nature are functional, structured, and goal-driven. GROW ticks all those boxes. The process helps in facilitating tangible outcomes; in other—words, it's functional. The four phases provide an easy to remember structure. And its goal orientation makes it ideal for the goal-driven manager. GROW is easy to remember, quick—to administer, and gets results.

Aside from the impromptu meeting, what about the structured, pre-planned coaching conversation?

GROW is suitable for pre-arranged coaching session too. One of the strengths of this model as I've stressed is that it provides a helpful structure for coaching. It also compels the leader to involve the participant in a collaborative coaching conversation. GROW is useful in all coaching contexts.

Although the GROW model is easy to use and applicable in most coaching circumstances, it requires a major shift in thinking. It essentially means moving from *telling* to *asking*. The keystone principle of the model is to support the coachee to determine their own answer to the dilemma, problem, or challenge they face. GROW is contradictory to the idea of the superior dictating to a subordinate. If telling is all that's required, the manager may as well send the team member an email with specific instructions!

A person's growth and development are fundamentally about them taking ownership and responsibility for their actions and results. By asking thought-provoking questions, the leader invites the coachee to do the thinking. The coachee is expected to be engaged in this type of coaching conversation. To foster ownership and responsibility, the leader asks challenging questions and listens intently to the team member's responses.

As I suggested in the previous chapter, the opportunities for quick, spontaneous coaching conversations (corridor conversations) occur daily. GROW focuses on solutions, facilitates learning, and nurtures positive change. Ask questions. Listen with intent. Clarify the next step. These are the hallmarks of a good coach.

In the next chapter, we consider the second developmental conversation: the delegation conversation.

The Top 10 Key Points …

1. GROW is a well-known coaching methodology. It stands for 'Goal,' 'Reality,' 'Options,' and 'What next?'
2. When someone comes to you with an issue, problem, or challenge and wants to 'dump' on you, politely stop them and ask: "What is the ideal outcome you are trying to achieve?"

3. Once they've explained what success looks like for them, you can then ask a different question: "What is getting in the way, or what is stopping you getting to this result?"
4. The next question for the leader is the hardest of all: "What options are open for you to resolving this?"
5. In the *Option* phase—like the other phases of GROW—the best strategy is to ask open-ended questions.
6. The 'W' is GROW stands for "What next?"
7. Following the GROW process, the appropriate course-of-action should now be clear.
8. GROW offers a simple, practical, and comprehensive framework for leaders to facilitate productive coaching conversations.
9. The GROW format reduces—not increases—time taken and teaches the employee to be self-sufficient. Self-sufficiency translates to less trivial interruptions for the manager.
10. Most organizational leaders are highly functional, structured, and goal-driven. GROW ticks all those boxes.

Notes

1. https://en.wikipedia.org/wiki/GROW_model#cite_note-1.
2. https://en.wiktionary.org/wiki/give_a_man_a_fish_and_you_feed_him_for_a_day;_teach_a_man_to_fish_and_you_feed_him_for_a_lifetime.

9

Conversation 2: The Delegation Conversation

Delegation is a driver of intrinsic motivation.

Russell Sy, managing director of a company that develops and manages business parks in the United Arab Emirates, learned how to delegate effectively from watching others. "I am fortunate to have a top-notch direct supervisor," *he says.* "Observing her delegate, motivate, and manage for results has taught me a lot." *But, like all of us, Russell has had both positive and negative experiences with delegation.*

In a previous role, he was assigned to lead a newly formed division. The CEO had combined five separate functions and asked Russell to ensure the integration went smoothly and saved the company money. Right off, he met with the five department heads to brainstorm how they would meet the CEO's mandate. He delegated several projects to each leader. Within a few weeks, he saw that one of the departments was falling behind and quickly assessed that the department head was the obstacle. The departmental head was unhappy with the amalgamation and thought it diminished his power-base, so he refused to cooperate. Eventually, Russell had to replace him. "I learned from this failure that it's important to delegate to someone who is genuinely on board," he says.

Now Russell looks for delegation opportunities that will benefit him, the direct report, and the organization. For example, when his company's parent group recently asked for a review of the business, he asked a new hire to prepare the information packet because he felt it was a great way to orient the employee. "Having a fresh pair of eyes look at our business uncovered a few blind spots."

Russell realizes trusting a newcomer with such an important task was a gamble. But he felt the risk could be mitigated by "instructions, open lines of communication for questions and comments, and regular checkpoints."[1]

Delegation is one of the most fundamental skills of effective management. And yet, the workshops I facilitate with managers consistently reveal it's one of the least used leadership capabilities. And this applies from senior executives through to supervisors. If you lead one or more people, learn to master delegation.

There are several reasons why we avoid or resist delegating. If this is an issue for you, then consider honestly why this is the case.

The delegation conversation advances the concept of human spirit and works only if it's done in the right way for the right reasons. The act of delegation should be a developmental learning experience. It should enable team member to broaden their perspective and grow their skills and capabilities. If it's done—on the other hand—just to off-load unpleasant work the manager doesn't want to do, that's an entirely different motivation. Done for this reason, the outcome is likely to be the opposite to engendering human spirit—it will probably generate human dispirit!

The proper basis for delegation can spark one's intrinsic motivation. We'll come back to this idea later. The delegation conversation is also consistent with the notion of workplace dignity. The leader—using delegation as a tool for growth—is supporting their team member to boost their sense of worth. Delegation is a sign of respect and can lift one's self-esteem, when done for the right reason.

A good delegation conversation honors the five pillars of authentic conversation. To delegate requires trust. It can further build trust once the team member demonstrates their capability and commitment over time. It can erode trust too, if the leader is let down! The leader should clarify their expectations and gain agreement from the team member on the outcome. Delegating shows appreciation by entrusting another person with the accomplishment of important work. The leader may, however, need to challenge unhelpful behavior along the way. And all delegation conversations are concerned with planning for the future. These are the five pillars in action.

Why Don't Managers Delegate?

Getting back to the question of why leaders don't delegate, here are some of the main reasons I've encountered.

One reason given to me frequently by managers is that they don't have anyone able or confident enough to delegate to. While this is undoubtedly true in some cases, using this as an excuse not to delegate doesn't resolve the matter of skill limitation. A leader must take a calculated risk occasionally and use delegation as a learning experience. Perhaps having a series of coaching conversations early on may minimize the risk. Once the employee's skills-set improves, then the leader's engagement can be more about delegation, than coaching. Developing people is central to leadership. And the delegation conversation is a great vehicle to do this.

Another reason I hear from managers for not delegating is that they don't think they have enough time to properly delegate a challenging task. The justification goes something like this: *By the time I have delegated an activity to someone else, I could have done it myself.* This is probably true—at least in the short term. But what about the long term?

Investing in delegation conversations ultimately saves time. By taking the time to delegate to a team member a task, activity, or project you currently do will eventually mean freeing you up from doing that work yourself. That extra time saved can be spent on core leadership duties. The delegation conversation saves you time, when you consider it this way. Ponder this: The more time you spend on some form of work you can rightly and successfully delegate, the more time you have to use more profitably elsewhere in the business. Granted, this requires an initial investment of time upfront in a delegation conversation with a trusted team member. But like any good investment, you reap the rewards later.

Yet another excuse some managers use is related to the hassle associated with delegation. These managers don't want to endure possible complaints from the employee delegated the task of being overworked or burdened. They don't want delegation to be perceived as dumping unwanted work on other people, in other words. With this kind of pressure hanging over the manager's head, they reason *It's just easier if I do it myself.* Further, they think the employee will just *grumble and think I'm lazy and wanting to off-load all my work onto them.* So, the best course-of-action with this burden is to abstain from delegating and do that task themselves.

Although, if we accept that the leader's primary role is to develop their people, leaders must delegate. Like the other nine conversations in this book, the delegation conversation is a growth opportunity. Apart from the prospect of extending people on the job, the manager's other primary responsibility is to get the work done they're responsible for, to an acceptable standard. This objective is achieved with and through other people. A manager must then have regular delegation conversations with team members. Worrying how others may react or feel about being given additional tasks is the wrong way to think.

Managers lament that they're time strapped—they never have enough time to complete their 'to-do' list. It reminds me of an old saying:

> We never have enough time to do everything. But we always have enough time to do the important things.

I can't remember who said this, but it makes perfect sense. It's not the volume of work we could do, but what we decide to tackle, that's key. Managing time is about managing priorities, in other words. Focusing on what's ultimately important is the name of the game. What are the time-consuming tasks that get in the way of concentrating on the leader's core responsibilities? is a significant question we need to consider on a regular basis.

These time-consuming—but vital—low leverage activities that are not core responsibilities of the leader are ripe for delegation. If handing these tasks onto someone else is challenging for you, talk to your manager. What are the tasks, activities, and projects you are currently doing that should be delegated to others? Ask your boss. Your manager will probably be helpful answering this question.

There's a time to delegate, and not to delegate. There are several considerations. One obvious factor is the person's readiness to take on more responsibility. When someone is ready to take ownership of a task, it'll probably frustrate them if you don't hand it over to them. It's also limiting for you not to take this opportunity to free up your time by delegating.

I'd like you to consider two other reasons for not delegating. These motives aren't easy to admit to. But they're limiting factors nonetheless. The first reason is enjoyment—the manager really enjoys doing the work. It's stimulating. It's fun. Or it suits their personality. While the manager knows they like the activity, they're not always ready to admit this as the reason for not delegating it. A manager might like organizing the annual Christmas party, for example. Is this activity the best use of their time? No. I'll bet it's not a line item in their job description. To an observer, this is something that ought to be done by someone else in the office, as enjoyable as it may be to organize.

Besides enjoyment, another reason for not delegating is a fear of losing control. Some managers micromanage to keep their finger on the pulse. This is born out of a feeling of insecurity. I remember asking a micromanager why he felt the need to micromanage. He claimed that having his finger on the pulse was important so that when his boss asked him a question, he would be able to answer it in a flash. He wanted to be seen to be across the detail of his department. Sounds like a plausible response, doesn't it? But as I reminded him, he could easily and effortlessly check out any situation with the press of a button and report back to his boss in a matter of minutes. Being in control and micromanaging aren't necessarily the same thing.

If you fail to delegate, you fail to fully develop others, and you fail to fully develop yourself. And the less you delegate, the less time you have available for developmental conversations with those you lead. Developmental conversations save time, not take time. So, you need to have delegation conversations.

The delegating conversation isn't about dumping work or responsibility on someone else, nor is it about abrogating your responsibilities. It's about incrementally increasing others' responsibility for their continual growth. We discussed the three key motivators at work: autonomy, mastery, and purpose in Chap. 2. Each dimension is connected to delegation. For instance,

- when responsibility is delegated, the recipient experiences more autonomy in how their work is done;
- when challenging tasks are delegated, the recipient's mastery is boosted; and
- when the recipient accepts the task, they are more aligned to the purpose of organizational work.

Delegation is a driver of intrinsic motivation.

Role clarity is enhanced too. Surveys indicate that a lack of role clarity is a reality in many cases. A thorough delegating conversation answer these four questions:

- What is being delegated, and what isn't?
- Who has the delegation and who needs to know that to ensure it's successful?
- What are the leader's expectations?
- Who is accountable for what?

The responses to these questions sharpen clarity.

Delegation doesn't mean delegating all responsibility for the task or project outcome. A delegation conversation isn't a one-off event—it ought to be frequent and ongoing, particularly for complex projects. You might choose to delegate one or two discrete aspects of a project or assignment. This approach can be useful to check out someone's readiness for additional responsibility. Delegate the task, but limit the authority through ongoing dialog. Ensure your team member doesn't run too far ahead of your span-of-control and accountability. For example, you can delegate the initial phase of a project, such as brainstorming, generating options, or researching fresh ideas for implementation. From here, you can then take over the rest of the project, or depending upon their readiness, involve them in the next phase. As much as we might worry about dumping work on others, many managers are carrying too many responsibilities that others could easily pick up (and maybe even do better!).

We often hear that delegating is too hard because it just takes too long to do. And there's no escaping the fact that delegation takes more time initially. It requires preparation, education, and evaluation—in short, it requires a conversation. If conversations are at the heart of the contemporary manager's work, the delegating conversation needs to be a regular part of a leader's communication. The delegation conversation is not only about your team members' development, it's also about your development as a leader too.

In the next chapter, I discuss 10 vital aspects of the delegation conversation that should be kept top-of-mind.

The Top 10 Key Points …

1. Delegation is one of the most fundamental skills of effective management.
2. The delegation conversation should be developmental; that is, one that helps the team member to grow skills and capabilities.
3. A good delegation conversation covers the five pillars of authentic conversation.
4. There are several psychological reasons why managers don't delegate.
5. Two powerful reasons that managers don't delegate is that that they enjoy the activity or want to retain the perception of control.
6. Time-consuming, low leverage activities are the places to start delegating.
7. If managers fail to delegate, they fail to fully develop others, and they fail to fully develop themselves.
8. The delegating conversation is not about dumping work or responsibility on someone else, nor is it about abrogating responsibility.

9. Because role clarity is such a frequent concern in organizational life, the delegating conversation can improve role clarity.
10. A delegation conversation isn't a one-off event—it ought to be frequent and ongoing, particularly for complex projects.

Note

1. Gallo, A. (2012). Why aren't you delegating? *Harvard Business Review*. https://hbr.org/2012/07/why-arent-you-delegating.

10

Ten Keys to a Better Delegation Conversation

> *The team member needs to understand what success looks like. But give them the freedom and autonomy to decide how best to go about achieving this outcome.*

We'll look at 10 key factors for successful delegation conversations in this chapter. Some of these vital aspects of delegation should be done (or not done) in the conversation itself, other factors should be considered before the delegation conversation, and others should be kept in mind as general principles. They're all important considerations nevertheless.

1. Freedom and Autonomy

Encourage the team member to decide how to tackle the delegated project themselves. This is preferable to telling the team member what needs to be done and how to do it. It's still important to explain what you expect at the end. The team member needs to understand what success looks like. But give them the freedom and autonomy to decide how best to go about achieving this outcome. There's nothing wrong with discussing their ideas on how they'll accomplish the project or task. Sometimes this can be a good conversation point, particularly when working in new terrain. But ultimately it should be left to the team member to figure out how the activity, task, or project ought to be done—that's part of the process of learning. Building safeguards around how and when you want to be informed of progress will ensure that the project won't go off the rails (see points 3 and 10).

One of the leader's most important tasks in the delegation conversation is to communicate the outcome they want achieved. It should follow the SMART formula. The outcome should be *Specific, Measurable, Action-based, Realistic,* and *Time-dated.* For example:

> I would like you to survey the entire membership of the organization in three months and produce a five-page report with a series of recommendations four weeks after that.

Notice that the goal is specific enough (*survey the entire membership of the organization*); action-based (*survey* and *produce*); measurable (*five-page report*); realistic and time-dated (*three months* and *four weeks*). If the team member is confused during the initial delegation conversation about the expected outcome, then the chances of them delivering the result you want is significantly limited.

2. Delegation of Authority

During the delegation discussion, you should clarify the extent and limits of the team member's authority in completing the task or project. The reason why this is important is that the activity will be outside the normal scope of the team member's responsibility. So, the team member's authority—at least for this exercise—needs to change too. Where are the new boundaries for the team member? What decisions can they make that are different to the normal work arrangements they have? are questions that need to be raised and answered early.

This different level of decision-making authority can be categorized with three questions:

- What doesn't change in the completion of this task?
- What does change in the completion of this task?
- What decisions might they make that they ordinarily don't have the authority to make?

Confirmation of what doesn't change should be agreed upon. Decisions that need to be made to get this task done outside the usual parameters of the team member's charter should be broached. The gray areas of potential confusion should be identified and discussed in the conversation.

3. Kept Informed

As I mentioned earlier, explain your expectation around being kept informed. More specifically, you should clarify what you need to be informed about, and what you don't need to be informed about. Also, the conversation ought to cover how often you should be informed of progress or challenges, and how you want to be informed. Should the updates be done informally or formally reported in the regular meeting schedule? How much detail do you require? and so on. This gives the team member confidence and certainty about the communication process.

In most cases, the leader—unless a micromanager—doesn't want or need to know everything. But at the same time, they don't want to be blindsided by an out-of-control bush fire.

4. Don't Interfere

Once you have delegated something to someone, get out of the way. Let them do what is now 'their job.' Don't make decisions in areas you have delegated to them. This is the epitome of micromanagement. Review progress and discuss options, but don't interfere! Let them do the job you delegated to them. If you've set up good systems of feedback and being kept informed and updated, this significantly minimizes the risk of something going off course.

By being informed and updated on a regular basis, an experienced leader can foreshadow potential problems. And if a problem is anticipated at one of these update meetings, this isn't a case of interfering. The issue can be discussed, and adjustments made. In these circumstances, use the GROW model you learnt in Chap. 7.

5. Don't Countermand

Worse than interfering unnecessarily, once a job has been delegated, is countermanding the team member. By countermanding, I mean overruling or taking the job off them and giving it to someone else, or doing it yourself. When a team member makes decisions in areas that you have delegated to them, don't stop them. By canceling, reversing, or ending a decision made by the team member, you are undermining their authority, and probably their confidence too. This sends a signal that you don't entirely trust them.

I understand that there are times when a leader must intervene in a project that they have delegated to someone else. In most cases, if it's explained properly, the team member will understand the need for your intervention too. For instance, the delegated project may carry with it some political sensitivities. And a politically sensitive area may justifiably require your involvement as a more senior manager. Done tactfully and sensibly with an explanation to the team member of why you need to get involved works a treat most times.

6. Delegating too Infrequently

It's always better to be accused of delegating too much than not enough. Unless there's an obvious and valid reason for doing the work, you should delegate it to someone else. This is usually easier said than done. But auditing what you do as a leader from time-to-time creates an awareness of some of the tasks that you are hanging on to and should let go. Ask yourself from time-to-time: *Why am I doing this task?*

If you're prepared to delegate more than you're currently doing, you'll be having more delegation conversations. In practice, this means you should be having delegation conversations daily, whether you have one or 1000 people reporting to you.

Engage a shadow, if it helps. Ask someone to watch you and to point out when they think you ought to be delegating. I think it's amusing and insightful that Ronald Reagan—arguably one of the most successful US Presidents—used to finish work at 5 pm each day in the White House and still manage a nap in the afternoon! President Reagan had this to say about delegation:

> Surround yourself with the best people you can find, delegate authority, and don't interfere as long as the policy you've decided upon is being carried out.[1]

I suppose President Reagan must have been good at delegating!

> **Where the Rubber Meets the Road …**
>
> **Leadership Advice from Ronald Reagan**
>
> Here is a short article from Matt Perman on former US President Ronald Reagan's leadership style:
>
> First, delegate *authority*–not tasks. I'm not saying there's no place for delegating tasks, but if that's your focus it won't scale. You should delegate *responsibility areas* and give people the authority to carry them out. (Responsibility in the final sense, of course, rests with the leader—he or she is the one ultimately accountable for results.)
>
> Second, that means that you consequently need to let your people act—if you keep interfering and micromanaging, you haven't truly delegated authority.
>
> Third, notice that Reagan didn't *simply* say "don't interfere." Which is interesting because the one main criticism of his leadership is that he was too hands-off. What he said was don't interfere *if the policy you decided on is being carried out*.
>
> There are defined outcomes. Let the person find their own way to accomplish them. If the policy that was decided on is not being carried out, then you need help the person make some course corrections.[2]

7. The Buck Stops with Me

Another great US President, Harry Truman, had the statement: *The buck stops with me* prominently placed on his Oval Office desk. It reminds us that the leader is ultimately the one responsible for what happens (or doesn't happen) in their sphere of influence. The team members you delegate to want and need to know that you will back them and support them, and in the end, take responsibility for the outcome. Taking responsibility for the outcome doesn't include taking the credit when it goes well, by the way! During the delegation conversations, it's important to reiterate to your team member that the buck stops with you. By taking overall accountability for the result doesn't mean the team member has no responsibility at all. They do. And it's important that these areas of liability are discussed with the team member.

8. Experience and Abilities

As I've said several times, consider the delegation conversation as a developmental opportunity, that is, a vehicle to develop the capabilities of team members. This implies that what you delegate ought to be challenging, but not too challenging that they will fall flat on their face. In other words, you shouldn't delegate beyond a point justified by a team member's experience or abilities.

When a manager delegates something that's beyond the scope of a colleague's capabilities, it can end in tears. If this happens, the manager inevitably blames the team member. *Why did he or she do that? Why didn't they talk to me? What's wrong with them? Why don't they listen?* and so on. But a finger-pointing manager conveniently forgets that it was their decision to delegate that work to an individual who was clearly out of their depths. That's the manager's mistake, not the team member's.

Often the team member themselves isn't the best judge of whether they can take on a new project or task. Ask them whether they think they are up to the challenge. But use your judgment too. People can underrate their capabilities. But others will overrate their ability too. It should ultimately be the manager's decision on whether the team member can meet a fresh test.

9. Don't Delegate only Routine Work

At the other end of the spectrum, only delegating routine work will stifle your people. There are times, of course, when delegating routine work is necessary. But the delegation conversation should—as we learnt earlier—be an exercise that is primarily aimed at developing the proficiencies of your team.

I think it's a good idea to explain to the delegatee that you are delegating a demanding body of work to support their growth and development. What's more, explain how you hope they will change in the process of successfully accomplishing the challenge. *What will they get from the experience? And how will it help them in their job and career?* are worth communicating.

10. Breathing Down Their Neck

It's not a good idea to breathe down a team member's neck after you've delegated the job to them. Breathing down someone's neck is another way of saying, *I need to check up on the team member.* This sends several negative signals to that person—it erodes their confidence. After all, the obvious signal in incessantly monitoring a team member's progress (or lack of progress) is that you don't have confidence in their ability to do the job. That's not edifying. A supplementary message you communicate by checking up too often is, *I'm micromanager and meddler!* Nobody likes to be micromanaged.

To mitigate this from happening, set some reporting guidelines early. (I discussed this in point 3). *How often? When? How?* are the questions to be resolved. How often do you want feedback? Once a week? Fortnightly? Establish this upfront and stick to the agreed schedule.

When is the best time to report progress? Early morning, afternoon. During the normal cycle of meetings? Again, commit to the agreement. How do you want this information conveyed to you? By report? Face-to-face? Email? Reporting on progress is an integral part of the delegation process. It may stop you from too many impromptu check-ups.

You would do well to be mindful of these 10 points when having your delegation conversations. Take your time. Think carefully about the conversation. Plan. And do it right the first time and you and the team member will reap the benefits.

This is the end of the chapter on the dos and don'ts of delegation. Delegation should be viewed as a developmental opportunity. It's a chance to help your team members grow and develop. There are several reasons why survey after survey shows that managers don't delegate enough. We've covered many of these reasons in the previous chapter. We've also covered some key points here for a better delegation experience. Delegation—like any conversation—is a dialog, rather than a monolog.

In the next chapter, we consider the visioning conversation.

The Top 10 Key Points …

1. Encourage the team member to decide how to tackle the delegated project themselves.
2. During the delegation discussion, you should clarify the extent and limits of the team member's authority in completing the task or project.
3. Explain your expectation around being kept informed.
4. Once you have delegated something to someone, get out of the way.
5. Worse than interfering unnecessarily once a job has been delegated to a team member, is countermanding the team member.
6. Unless there's an obvious and valid reason for doing the work, you should delegate it to someone else.
7. The leader is ultimately the one responsible for what happens (or doesn't happen) in their area of responsibility.
8. Delegate a challenging assignment for the team member, but not too challenging that they will fall flat on their face.

9. Delegate routine tasks sparingly.
10. It's not a good idea to breathe down the team member's neck after you have delegated the job to them.

Notes

1. Perman, M. (2009). Leadership advice from Ronald Reagan. https://www.whatsbestnext.com/2009/11/leadership-advice-from-ronald-reagan/.
2. Ibid.

11

Conversation 3: The Visioning Conversation

We all crave a sense of purpose and meaning in what we do.

Marina, a young law graduate with a passion for social justice and humanitarian care, took a holiday job with World Vision, promoting child sponsorship and aid donations in shopping centers. It's hard, repetitive work that involves a lot of rejection, from averted eyes to outright refusal and occasional accusations of wasted money. Nevertheless, the young graduate's passion remained undimmed after months of this work. Why? Because the World Vision marketing team regularly and frequently gathered their team members to share experiences, celebrate successes, take input, and remind them of the purpose of the work they were doing. Their job is not simply about getting sponsorships, but about upholding World Vision's profile and using the opportunities for advocacy of the valuable work the organization does.[1]

What's a visioning conversation? Why is it important? And what are some chief considerations for these conversations? In the world we live in, we are bombarded with a never-ending surge of information coming from all directions at warp speed. It's off-putting, distracting, and mesmerizing, all at the same time. It's never been easier to be sidetracked—it can be done in the blink of an eye. A lot of the time we don't even realize we've been diverted off course, until it's too late. This is where the visioning conversation helps—it can cut through the clutter of the dynamic work-setting. The purpose of the visioning conversation is to keep people on the straight and narrow.

People need more than ever a sense of clarity and purpose in the work they do and in their personal lives. *What's important? What's not? What's changed? Where are we heading? What do I need to do now and in the future?* are the questions the visioning conversation addresses. Investing time in these questions is imperative for leaders and their colleagues. One of the leader's roles is to help people see the forest, and not just the trees.

Leadership gurus, James Kouzes and Barry Posner, gave us the five practices of exemplary leaders.[2] Two of those practices are *inspire a shared vision* and *encourage the heart*.[3] In this chapter, we'll explore the first practice and in Chap. 13 we'll discuss the encouraging conversation—a way of cultivating their second practice.

Vision can sound like a lofty concept, but it's an everyday need we have in our work and personal lives. We all crave a sense of purpose and meaning in what we do. Simon Sinek reminds us in his book, *Start with Why: How Great Leaders Inspire Everyone to Take Action*, that "it doesn't matter what you do, it matters why you do it."[4] He explains that while most companies talk about *what* they do or make—and *how* they go about it—few articulate the most powerful thing: *why* they do what they do. And it's the *why* that inspires.

The visioning conversation very much connects human spirit with work. People need to see the big picture—they covet a believable future. Most employees naturally want to know why we are doing something and how it contributes to the strategic direction and values of the enterprise. Managers sadly assume employees can connect the dots between a mundane task and its ultimate purpose. People generally have trouble making this connection.

Here's a simple example of what a leader can do to help a team member connect the dots.

Consider the routine task of sweeping the floor in the production area of a business. As mundane as it is, it can be put into a positive context. The production supervisor points out to the seemingly blasé sweeper that the company is hosting an important potential customer after the shift. The company wants to make the very best impression possible on this important visitor. If the right impression is made—which includes the tidiness of the production area—it may result in this customer being persuaded to place a significant order of product worth millions of dollars a year. Everyone has a role to play in winning this customer's business, including the person asked to sweep the floor of the production area. An explanation along these lines provides background to what would otherwise appear an insignificant task. The employee then knows and values the higher purpose, beyond sweeping the floor.

Imagine for a moment the difference it could make if all business leaders—for every task, big and small—explained the *why*. What a difference it would make to inspire higher levels of intrinsic motivation.

Communicating purpose can be done in many ways. It can involve sharing some positive customer feedback, or illustrating how the end-user benefits from the products or services employees make or provide. But managers don't communicate purpose enough for two main reasons—the extra time it takes and the assumption that the employee already *gets it*. Granted, employees in certain industries—such as the not-for-profit sector—have an easier time valuing the connection between their work and the tangible results of that work in the community. But with a little thought, an appreciation of its effectiveness, and taking the time to explain the overriding purpose, leaders can make a substantial contribution in creating a heady motivational environment. This creates the right setting for human spirit to flourish.

We discussed the relevance of *purpose* in Chap. 2. It's one of the intrinsic drivers of motivation. The challenge for leaders is to turn rudimentary tasks into more meaningful activities. The visioning conversation is one way to communicate this.

What this means in practice is explaining the superseding purpose of a task, project, and activity. When asking someone to complete any type of work—regardless of how routine or trivial it is—the leader should at the very least explain the consequences of doing (and not doing) the job well. Managers shouldn't make the mistake of assuming all employees comprehend the consequences of the work they do—they often don't.

When people are asked to do jobs that are commonplace, it shows some dignity to them by explaining the worth of the work that needs doing.

A visioning conversation touches on the five pillars of authentic conversation. It builds trust by giving the team member a sense of the wider landscape. The conversation helps them to see the big picture and the leaders' expectations supporting that end. By couching a task in a broader context, they are showing appreciation for the job-holder and the work they do. Behaviors that are inconsistent with the leaders' vision can be justifiably challenged when the vision is clearly articulated. And it stands to reason that the visioning conversation is all about the future.

One of the fundamentals of leadership is having and sharing an inspiring vision of the future. Communicating with vision fundamentally responds to the question: *Why are we doing this task or project?* More specifically, sharing a vision considers these three questions:

- Why does this (job, task, project) make a difference?
- Why is the team member's contribution important?
- Why is it important to do it right and be accountable?

You might like to check out one of my other books—*The New Influencing Toolkit: Capabilities to Communicate with Influence*,[5] to further appreciate the power of *why*.

It's easy to think of the visioning conversation as something like a motivating half-time exhortation by a coach. But it's worth thinking about what motivates us when we are conversing with our leaders. It's usually less about some grand strategy in which we're a small cog, than about our interest in our own contribution—particularly when we have a concern, complaint, or suggestion. Attention, listening, and empathy are key ingredients in any good conversation and crucial to ensuring genuine dialog in any relationship, team, or organization. Kouzes and Posner elaborate on this:

> As counterintuitive as it might seem, then, the best way to lead people into the future is to connect with them deeply in the present. The only visions that take hold are shared visions—and you will create them only when you listen very, very closely to others, appreciate their hopes, and attend to their needs. The best leaders are able to bring their people into the future because they engage in the oldest form of research: They observe the human condition.[6]

We look to our leaders for a sense of what the future holds—how strengths can be utilized, how weaknesses can be minimized or overcome, how threats will be dealt with, how opportunities will be realized, and how we will remain viable and healthy. This forward-looking perspective is one of the key leadership traits Kouzes and Posner have identified from their 25 years of research.

Storytelling is another powerful but frequently ignored communication tool for sharing the vision and emphasizing the relevance of our work. Stories embrace the heart, they tap into our visual memory and emotions, and personalize otherwise remote ideas. As far back as Aristotle, communicators have been advised to speak not only to the head, but to the heart *(pathos)*. Rob Goffee, professor of organizational behavior at London Business School, and Gareth Jones, former director of HR and Internal Communication at the BBC, consider the power of meaning and stories in organizational life in their book *Why Should Anyone Be Led by You?*

> The mistake many leaders make is to assume that followers can be engaged primarily through rational analysis and straightforward assertion of facts … But this approach—on its own—is rarely successful in energising others … In order to properly engage others, leaders need to construct a compelling narrative. They must find a way of looking at the world that allows others not only to understand their role in it but also to be excited by it.[7]

Seeking out and sharing stories that illustrate the organization's vision and values-in-action can be rousing.

The visioning conversation is an opportunity for you to discuss your vision, goal, or destination so that your team not only get it, but wholeheartedly embrace it. To successfully impart vision is to stimulate an emotional attachment to that vision. Understanding a vision is one thing, but to be excited by it is entirely another thing. Comprehending it is logical. Being inspired by it is emotional. Both can be achieved in conversation.

In a nutshell, the visioning conversation is about expressing and sharing the leader's vision. Numerous studies have shown that leaders who enthusiastically promote and communicate their vision tend to create the positive effects on employee performance, attitudes, and perspectives. It creates the right environment for employees to perform. To successfully communicate a vision, a leader needs to do three things well:

- They should display a dynamic and confident communication style;
- They need to act to support the implementation of the vision; otherwise, it is literally just a set of words; and
- The leader's role is to build the confidence of people to believe they can significantly contribute to the vision.

An inspiring vision communicated well moves people.

To assist you with what might seem a daunting prospect, we'll consider two easy to implement tools in the next chapter. First, I'll provide you with a set of questions to facilitate a coherent vision collaboratively with your team. And second, I'll share with you an effective tool I refer to as a "Team Values Charter." We consider these two tools in the context of promoting an emotional connection to the vision through the medium of conversation.

Visioning is an important process that provides focus. It shows what to aim for and builds a pathway to its achievement. A vision is a picture in words of what the leader wants to achieve. Communicating a vision is important in sharing ownership and developing commitment.

The Top 10 Key Points …

1. People need more than ever a sense of clarity and purpose in their work the work they do and in their personal lives.
2. The visioning conversation very much connects human spirit with work.

3. Communicating purpose can be done in many ways.
4. We all crave a sense of purpose and meaning in what we do.
5. One of the fundamentals of leadership is having and sharing an inspiring vision of the future.
6. We look to our leaders for a sense of what the future holds—how strengths can be utilized, how weaknesses can be minimized or overcome, how threats will be dealt with, how opportunities will be realized, and how we will remain viable and healthy.
7. Stories are a frequently ignored means of sharing the vision and value of what a team or organization is doing.
8. The visioning conversation is about expressing and sharing the leader's vision.
9. Visioning is an important process to give team members a focus.
10. Numerous studies have shown that leaders who enthusiastically promote and communicate their vision tend to create positive effects on employee performance, attitudes, and perceptions.

Notes

1. Baker, T. & Warren, A. (2015). *Conversations at work: Promoting a culture of conversation in the changing workplace.* London: Palgrave Macmillan.
2. Kouzes, J. & Posner, B. (1987). The leadership challenge: How to make extraordinary things happen in organizations. Wiley.
3. Kouzes, J. & Posner, B. (2007). *The leadership challenge* (4th ed.). Jossey-Bass.
4. Sinek, S. (2011). Start with Why: How great leaders inspire everyone to take action. Penguin.
5. Baker, T.B. (2015). *The new influencing toolkit: Capabilities to communicate with influence.* London: Palgrave Macmillan.
6. Kouzes, J. and Posner, B. (2009). To lead, create a shared vision *Harvard Business Review* (January). http://hbr.org/2009/01/to-lead-create-a-shared-vision/ar/1.
7. Goffee, R. & Jones, G. (2006). Why should anyone be led by you? Boston, MA: Harvard Business School Press.

12
Visioning Tools for Group and Individual Conversations

> *Ideally everything that is said, done, and thought about in an organization ought to be consistent with the vision—or at the least, not contradictory with the vision.*

In this chapter, we consider two powerful tools for facilitating visioning conversations. They can be used in both one-to-one or group situations. These tools are easy to use and can have a very positive impact with the right people, at the right time.

Six Visioning Questions

By answering six questions, the leader can focus their thoughts and the collective thoughts of their team on creating a vision:

1. *Why* does our organization/department/team exist?
2. *Who* are our customers/important stakeholders?
3. *Where* are our customers/important stakeholders, and *what* do they value?
4. *What* industry or business/activity is our organization in?
5. In *what* industry or business/activity will our organization be in the future?
6. *How* are we different from our competition?

Being able to answer these questions offers a sound starting point for developing a vision. This exercise as I said can be used either individually or collectively in a one-on-one or group format. You can use it to get your priorities right as a leader. Or, you can ask these questions to prompt a discussion with your immediate team or a single team member. If you're the CEO, the six visioning questions can be thrashed out with your senior management team, although this exercise can be conducted anywhere within an organization or, with any team. Regardless of where a leader asks these questions, it helps to get clarity around the direction of people's work.

> **2. Where the Rubber Meets the Road …**
>
> **A Vision Is Like a Coat Hanger**
>
>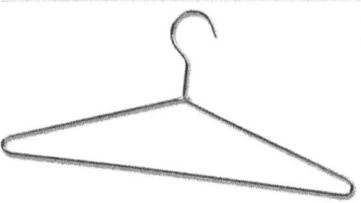
>
> I think of a vision statement as a coat hanger in a closet. We all have too many coat hangers, right? They sometimes seem like they breed!
>
> In any case, they're pretty much useless on their own—they can even be downright annoying. So too can a vision statement hanging on a wall be annoying—no-one pays it much attention and it normally just takes up space.
>
> However, the coat hanger is very useful for hanging garments off. In fact, the coat hanger helps to shape the item of clothing hanging off it. This is what a vision statement that employees are emotionally attached to does. Ideally everything that is said, done, and thought about in an organization ought to be consistent with the vision—or at the least, not contradictory with the vision. The way we approach our work; the way we treat each other and our important stakeholders and customers; the way we problem-solve; the way we reward each other; the way we measure our success, and so on can be evaluated looking through the prism of the vision statement.
>
> In sum, a vision is a critically important declaration that's used to guide and inform every decision organizational members make.[1]

Team Values Charter

A *team values charter* is a persuasive tool to support a team to work together toward a common purpose. It's not a time-consuming exercise. But nonetheless, it can be very insightful. It's best done face-to-face with all team members present, but can work remotely, if necessary.

Here's how it works.

At the beginning of a meeting the leader asks each person in the team to respond in writing to five questions. It's important that team members write down their responses to each question. It's also imperative that the team leader participates too. The leader wants their team members to have thought clearly and deeply about these questions; writing responses helps in this regard. This isn't an exercise that should be done off-the-cuff.

Here are the five questions:

1. *What* one value is important to you when functioning in this team?
2. *What* does this value mean to you?
3. *Why* is this value important to you?
4. *What* type of behaviors would violate this value?
5. *What* type of behaviors would be consistent with this value?

To illustrate, here is an example of someone's responses to the five questions:

1. What one value is important to you when functioning in this team?

   Respect.

2. What does this value mean to you?

   Respect to me means being prepared to listen to another point-of-view from a team member in an open and non-judgmental way even if you don't necessarily agree with their perspective.

3. Why is this value important to you?

   This value of respect is important to me because I believe we ought to be encouraging diversity in the way we think and operate as a team. And if we are prepared to respect the views of others that we don't necessarily agree with, it will encourage others to speak up.

4. What type of behaviors would violate this value?

   I think someone interrupting another colleague before he or she has finished fully expressing their point-of-view is inappropriate. In my mind, this is disrespectful.

5. What type of behaviors would be consistent with this value?

   Actively listening to a different point-of-view with respect and interest.

After everyone has completed their written responses, the leader invites each person to share their answers to the five questions with the rest of the team. It's a good idea for the leader to start the conversation by verbalizing their responses; this should set a positive tone for the exercise.

As each team member is offering their perspective, the leader encourages colleagues to ask questions of the presenter for clarification. This should be an interactive discussion and not a series of static presentations. The more interaction and informality in the room the better.

Once everyone has responded to these five questions, the team has effectively obtained the content necessary to create a team values charter. If there are six members in the team including the team leader, and each person has a different value, the team values charter will have six values and a defining statement for each value.

Instead, if more than one person has the same value; for example, *respect*, then the two or more team members work together to come up with a defining statement that captures their collective thoughts on that value. The key point here is that everyone in the team has input into the composition of the charter.

When the wording in the definition of the value is clear and reflects the sentiments of the contributing team member(s), the team values charter can be framed and put on the wall of the regular meeting room. The charter can also be distributed and displayed prominently on the desktops of the six team members as a reminder of their agreement to each other.

This exercise is very simple. But don't be fooled by its simplicity. It's enormously potent. The team members are emotionally connected to this charter because a value they strongly believe in is embedded in this document. Put it this way: Team members genuinely *own* the charter. And because of this sense of ownership, team members are much more likely to stick to it. You may find that from time-to-time members of the team start to hold each other accountable for their team values. This is of course a positive development.

From a leadership perspective, you now have a tool that expands your influence via conversation. How so? You too can—and should—hold the team (and yourself) accountable to your team values charter. The charter is a shared vision of how the team wants to work together. By applying this tool, the leader has effortlessly led the team to design their own vision of how they see themselves operating as a team. The team has also offered a set of values for you to hold the team accountable for their behavior and actions in their daily interactions with one another.

When a new member joins your team, they should be invited to contribute their responses to the five questions. The charter is then updated to include their value and associated definition. If this new team member is replacing someone else in the team, it's very important in my view that the previous team member's value remain in the charter. It sends a signal to the remaining members of the team that their contribution is also important and will be honored when they too move on.

So, this brings us to the end of the chapter on the two visioning tools—one that considers the external environment and the other, the interactions between team members. We discussed in the previous chapter what a visioning conversation is and why it's relevant. In this chapter we looked at two tools.

As a quick recap: This conversation is essentially about discussing with someone the value of the task they are undertaking. The visioning conversation puts the work of people into a team or organizational context. The visioning conversation can connect one's human spirit with the work they do. If a person understands the relevance of the work, they do—no matter how mundane it may appear on the surface—it can tap an intrinsic desire to do the job well. We've just covered two visioning methods. The first was using several questions to articulate a collective vision. And the second way is to create a vision of how the team want to interact with each other. Both work very well from my experience, if done thoroughly, and not in an ad hoc manner.

In the next chapter, we shall look at the encouraging conversation.

The Top 10 Key Points …

1. By answering the following six questions, the leader can focus their thoughts and the collective thoughts of their team on creating a vision.
2. The visioning questions exercise can be used either individually or collectively in a one-on-one or group format.
3. The six vision questions help bring clarity to the direction of people's work.
4. A team values charter is a persuasive tool to support a team to work together toward a common purpose.
5. The team values charter is based on team members' answering five key questions.
6. The team values charter is an interactive exercise, usually done as a team conversation.
7. Everyone in the team has an input into the team values charter.
8. When the wording is right, the team values charter can be framed and put on the wall of the regular meeting room.

9. The team members are emotionally connected to this charter because a value they strongly believe in is embedded in the document.
10. The team values charter is a common vision of how the team wants to work together.

Note

1. Baker, T.B. (2015). The new influencing toolkit: Capabilities for communicating with influence. London: Palgrave Macmillan.

13

Conversation 4: The Encouraging Conversation

Showing a genuine interest and care for others is the starting point for great leadership.

When Rob took over a team dispersed across the region, his management style of regular face-to-face interactions to provide a constant flow of feedback, recognition, and appreciation was challenged by distance and separation. Telephoning people sometimes worked, but of course they weren't always available—and he worried about catching them at a bad time for what he considered important messages. So, he reluctantly resorted to email on occasion.

An early experience was hearing of a positive initiative taken by a remote employee. He drafted an email simply saying he'd been told about it and expressing his appreciation for the work that Helen had done. He was later simultaneously pleased and concerned by what he heard about Helen after receiving his message. Pleased because she was so happy about it. Helen printed it out and posted it at their desk, even pointing it out to colleagues who dropped by. It was such a big deal—a completely new experience for Helen (and her colleagues) to receive a simple note of recognition and appreciation from their manager.[1]

Encouraging someone at work can engender human spirit. Encouragement promotes self-sufficiency, builds capacity, and provides context—all intrinsic motivational forces. It's dignifying to acknowledge, reassure, and inspire team members. Further, it develops trust, clarifies expectations, expresses appreciation, encourages desirable behavior, and focuses on a better future. In a nutshell, the encouraging conversation is authentic.

When I get the opportunity to talk with employees privately, they often say they'd like more encouragement from their boss. Managers don't always appreciate the need to be encouraging. They often assume that having an encouraging conversation with a team member doesn't have any real benefit. And not surprisingly, there are too few encouraging conversations at work. The encouraging conversation is underrated. Yet, it can have enormous impact when communicated authentically.

There's a saying attributed to former US President Theodore Roosevelt that,

> Nobody cares how much you know until they know how much you care.

But no known source can be found to verify the attribution. Anyway, I think it's an insightful and true statement, regardless. Remember: All the power and persuasive technique can fail us if we neglect the very real power of emotion in the way we communicate with people. Showing a genuine interest and care for others is the starting point for great leadership.

I think some managers have the misguided belief that showing warmth, giving praise, and exhibiting a caring attitude will somehow adversely affect employee performance. These managers rationalize that the team member may go 'soft', loose their edge, or lower their standards. Nonsense. Encouragement will more likely do the opposite, if done authentically. Being supportive undoubtedly builds resilience, improves performance, and boosts effort.

Opportunities to engage in encouraging conversations are perhaps among the easiest to identify in our working relationships. They're certainly among the most pleasant! A key to bringing out the best in others is to express appreciation, acknowledge contributions, and celebrate achievements. Sincere recognition is a powerful motivator. It feeds our human need for significance. "Followers want to feel significant," say leadership authors Goffee and Jones. They elaborate:

> In simple terms, they need recognition for their contribution. Social psychologists have made repeated pronouncements on this profound human need for recognition. So it is remarkable how often as individuals we seem to want it but not give it.[2]

Perhaps it's a fear that our praise will be rejected that holds us back. Or maybe there's something in our psyche (or organizational culture) that says we need to be 'hard' rather than 'soft'. Whatever those misconceptions might be, if you want to have quality conversations, then regular affirmation, recognition, and appreciation needs to be present. There's plenty of research that shows our human need for 'positivity', and that maintaining a realistically positive perspective helps us be more creative and productive.

> **Where the Rubber Meets the Road**
>
> **How Positivity Affects our Brains**
>
> How do positive and negative emotions work in our brains, and what we can learn from that?
>
> Positive emotions generally work in an opposite way to negative emotions. So, while emotions like fear, anxiety, stress, and anger narrow our focus, inhibit our concentration, and decrease our cognitive abilities, positive emotions can do the opposite. When we're feeling upbeat and happy, we're more likely to have an inclusive focus than a self-centered outlook, and to perform better on cognitively demanding tasks.
>
> That is why exercising often makes us happier, especially if we choose to go for a demanding workout.
>
> In the face of negative events, our brains struggle to perform at their highest–or even normal–capacity. Our prefrontal cortex, the brain's "executive center" is pushed aside so the amygdala can take over and prepare the body for crisis.
>
> This shift in control to the low road favors automatic habits, as the amygdala draws on knee-jerk responses to save us.
>
> When we're stressed or scared, for instance, we struggle to think clearly, to coordinate well with others, to take in new information and to come up with new ideas. Even existing routines suffer, as our concentration is taken over by our negative emotions.
>
> The more intense the pressure, the more our performance and thinking will suffer.
>
> In his book *Social Intelligence: The New Science of Human Relationships*, Daniel Goleman explains that heightened prefrontal activity, which is associated with positive emotions, enhances mental abilities such as "creative thinking, cognitive flexibility, and the processing of information." The left prefrontal area of our brains, which lights up with activity when we're in a positive mood, is also associated with reminding us of the good feelings we'll have when we reach a long-term goal.[3]

Thank-you

One of the simplest, most effective and yet most neglected way to encourage can be expressed in two words: *thank-you*. Thank-you for showing such initiative; thank-you for staying back late to complete that project; thank-you for speaking up yesterday during the meeting and expressing your point-of-view; thank-you for dealing with that customer so professionally under difficult circumstances. Like all useful feedback, if it's done in the right place, at the right time, in the right way, with the right intention, to the right person, it will be a source of encouragement.

Learn to say thank-you more often. Do it genuinely. In face-to-face situations make eye contact with the other person when you are saying thank-you. You will find it's appreciated and you'll feel better too. It's part of the encouraging conversation. Explain what the thank-you is for. *Thank-you for maintaining your cool under the pressure of that trying customer. Thank-you for staying back two hours on Friday evening to complete that report.* No one will ever complain that you say thank-you too much.

Here is a simple and potent exercise to illustrate my point. For the next week, starting tomorrow, commit to having three brief conversations every day that are encouraging. If nothing else, it forces you to look for things that merit encouragement. Managers are very good at spotting situations in the workplace that are going wrong and feel a sense of obligation to point out these occurrences to employees. You can continue with this. It's part of your job as a leader. But try balancing it up with identifying three opportunities for having encouraging conversations. If you aren't used to this approach, and genuine in your endeavor, you will be amazed at the positive impact of these conversations on morale, engagement, motivation, and general good-will in your team.

Encouragement and Engagement

You can't go a day without hearing or reading about the benefits of engaged employees. Why is there so much attention and focus on employee engagement? Well, it's pretty straight forward: When engagement increases within a company, productivity, profitability, and employee retention increase as well. Some of the pre-eminent studies about employee engagement come from the *Gallup Corporation*. One of the areas of expertise Gallup is known for is its "Q12"—12 survey questions used to measure the level of employee engagement, which were developed in the mid-1990s, and are still relevant today.

Many of these 12 questions focus on the direct impact a leader has on the level of employee engagement. I would like to look at these questions and consider the role of the encouraging conversation in promoting employee engagement.

Here are the 12 questions[4]:

1. Do I know what is expected of me at work?
2. Do I have the materials and equipment I need to do my work right?
3. At work, do I have the opportunity to do what I do best every day?

4. In the last seven days, have I received recognition or praise for doing good work?
5. Does my supervisor, or someone at work, seem to care about me as a person?
6. Is there someone at work who encourages my development?
7. At work, do my opinions seem to count?
8. Does the mission/purpose of my company make me feel my job is important?
9. Are my co-workers committed to doing quality work?
10. Do I have a best friend at work?
11. In the last six months, has someone at work talked to me about my progress?
12. This last year, have I had opportunities at work to learn and grow?

You will notice that Q.6 specifically mentions encouragement. Yet, I would suggest all 12 questions are related to encouragement. For an employee to respond positively to each of the 12 questions and therefore display a high level of engagement, their leader would need to demonstrate skill, ability, and empathy to encourage this team member. On that basis, I would like to review each theme in the 12 questions briefly in the next chapter, considering how a leader can create an affirmative response from team members to the Q12.

The Top 10 Key Points …

1. Encouraging someone at work can engender human spirit.
2. It's dignifying to acknowledge, reassure, and inspiring team members.
3. Employees often say they want more encouragement at work. Managers don't always appreciate the need to be encouraging.
4. Some managers have the misguided belief that showing warmth, encouragement, and a caring attitude will somehow adversely affect employee performance.
5. Opportunities to engage in encouraging conversations are perhaps among the easiest to identify in our working relationships.
6. One of the simplest, most effective, and yet most neglected way to encourage can be expressed in two words: thank-you.
7. Learn to say thank-you more often.
8. There is a link between encouragement and engagement.

9. Gallup's 'Q12' measures the level of employee engagement and is based on 12 questions.
10. The Q12 all have some basis in encouragement.

Notes

1. Baker, T.B. & Warren, A. (2015). Conversations at work: Promoting a culture of conversation in the changing workplace. London: Palgrave Macmillan.
2. Goffee, R. & Jones, G. (2006). Why should anyone be led by you? Boston: Harvard Business School Press.
3. Goleman, D. (2006). Social intelligence: The new science of human relationships. London: Hutchinson.
4. https://christopherfeld.wordpress.com/2011/02/03/gallups-12-questions-to-measure-employee-engagement/.

14

Twelve Powerful Ways to Engage or Disengage People at Work

> *At its most basic, organizations are a collection of people working in a structured way towards a common goal.*

A useful framework to consider when encouraging team members is the Q12 I introduced in the last chapter. In this chapter, I want to expand upon these 12 questions and consider ways to include these ideas in your conversations as a means of encouragement.

Expectations

Leaders set and communicate their expectations to team members. Employees need to understand what is expected of them. Without clear expectations, people can understandably feel anxious and unsure.

One of the five pillars of authentic conversations I covered in Chap. 5 is *Agree on expectations* (Pillar 2). Leaders need to be sure about their expectations, communicate those expectations clearly, and gain commitment that they will be met. Performance expectations provide the foundation for encouraging people toward meeting outcomes. And if these results are achieved, thanking them for doing so.

The encouraging conversation reminds the team member of the leader's standards. The leader should inspire them to stretch if necessary to meet those expectations. And a thank-you when they do, is always well received.

Materials and Equipment

To achieve optimal performance—with full engagement—people require the right resources. Adequate resourcing is encouraging. The opposite is true too: When resources are limited, it's discouraging. With substandard materials and equipment, it's like having one arm tied behind your back in a fight. Inferior working conditions, poor or outdated equipment, and unsafe work practices all fall under this category. Not only will not having the right materials and equipment adversely influence performance, it negatively impacts engagement too.

The encouraging conversations should consider organizational support. The conversation ought to contemplate the materials and equipment resources and tools the team member is using or expected to use to do the job. I acknowledge that sometimes it isn't possible to support an employee with the latest and greatest tools. But the conversation can at least consider how they can best manage with the resources they have available and what you can do to support them. With clear expectations and the right tools, the employee is off to a good start.

Opportunity

Ideally, people should be given the opportunity to do what they do best every day. *Are team members exercising their natural strengths in the current work they do? What can you do to foster the innate talents of people?* Sometimes it's not possible to do anything about this. But discussing strengths can create an awareness to look for future opportunities that complement an employee's strong suit.

You can explore these opportunities and stimulate consciousness and commitment to enable the team member to play to their strengths. That's encouraging. Often the leader is in the best position to objectively observe strengths and talents in others. You can encourage team members to exercise these traits in their day-to-day work, wherever possible. For example, someone who is naturally gifted in dealing with demanding customers ought to be stimulated to have more customer interaction or coach others. Good leaders encourage others to give their best and support them in that pursuit.

Recognition

Recognition and positive reinforcement is sparse, as we know. It's used sparingly everywhere, not just at work. Organizational psychologists keep tell us that most people need positive reinforcement and encouragement to flourish at work. Knowing what's expected, having the right tools, and playing to people's strengths, is a good start to being encouraged at work. People are responsive to recognition too.

Recognition can be planned or spontaneous. Planned recognition could be a presentation or announcement at a designated meeting. Spontaneous recognition is when the leader acknowledges good work privately. Recognizing someone can—and should—be an integral part of the encouraging conversation.

Conversations provide a great opportunity for leaders to acknowledge the good work people do.

When giving any positive feedback three 'rules' apply:

- Be specific about what you're recognizing;
- Be genuine; and
- Explain the positive impact the behavior had on the work environment.

Caring

At its most basic, organizations are a collection of people working in a structured way toward a common goal. With that thought in mind, managers lead people who are job-holders, not the other way around; that is, managers leading job-holders who happen to be people! People usually respond well to leaders who authentically show they care—treating people as individuals, in other words. To recap: Clarifying expectations, providing good working conditions (wherever possible), using people's talents (wherever possible), and recognizing their efforts are all characteristics of encouragement. We can now add: *Caring*, to the list. Showing you care for people who work for you can be done (or not done) in a variety of ways.

Having an encouraging conversation is one of the best ways to demonstrate genuine care for your colleagues. Taking a genuine interest in the employee and their family shows interest and a sense of care, for example. Empathizing with the inevitable life challenges employees go through from time-to-time displays a caring attitude too. These things count.

Development

Supporting a team member in their personal and technical development is another important responsibility of leadership. As the workplace is in a perpetual state of flux, so too should employees be in a state of constant learning and development. Growth and development ought to be top-of-mind for everyone.

People need to keep pace in the rapidly changing world of work. Organizations are morphing and changing, and employees too should upskill to keep up with these transformations. Clear expectations, the right resources, capitalizing on strengths, acknowledging good work, and showing care and interest are all elements of encouragement we have covered so far. An engaging leader also takes an active interest in the development of the people they lead.

An encouraging conversation can be based on the development of the employee. You might like to check out Chap. 22 for more guidance. Depending upon how it's done, discussing ways and means of improving aspects of the work employees do now and in the future is encouraging.

Opinions

People appreciate it when they know their opinions count for something. The reverse is true: People become very disengaged when their opinions are ignored or dismissed as irrelevant. Asking people for their opinion is a way of showing appreciation and respect. The twenty-first-century workplace is more collaborative than it once was. Younger employees expect to have some say in the decision-making process; they expect their manager to ask for their opinion on many workplace issues. Millennials may not have the answers, but they expect to be consulted!

In sum, leaders ought to clarify expectations, make sure employees have the right tools to do the job, utilize their strong points, praise and recognize good work, show empathy and be caring. We can now add: Take an interest in people's opinions.

Taking an interest in the opinions of others means leaders inviting team members to share their opinion about matters at work. Good leaders not only seek out the opinions of others, they value those opinions too. *What do you think about …? I'm interested in your view on …? Which direction would you take …?* These are question starters that encourage people to offer their opinion.

Relevance

How relevant an individual feels their job is can have a significant bearing on their level of engagement. On the flip side, if an employee thinks their job is relatively insignificant and unimportant, it diminishes their energy levels.

But if someone believes their role is meaningful to the success of the business, they're more likely to be engaged. As I've indicated throughout this book, it's the leader's responsibility to articulate the relevance of the individual's contribution to the overall success of the business. Too often the leader assumes—wrongly—that the job-holder understands the worth of their job in the full spectrum of business activity. They often don't understand.

One of the most effective—yet least utilized—ways of encouraging an employee is to explain the impact of their role in the organization. People want to know and feel they have relevance. This can be done in two ways. You can point out to the employee the negative consequences of not doing their job properly. Or talk about how a good job significantly results in a positive outcome, even indirectly. Use critical incidents in both cases. Discuss projects, workplace events, and activities and their impact in the scheme of things. Talk about the interdependencies of how one event or incident can, and does, influence other conditions in the business. By doing this, you are expressing the relevance and meaning of the employee's role in the overall success of the business.

Commitment

Showing commitment to their work is characteristic of an engaged employee. As we know only too well, not everyone feels committed to their work. Nonetheless, you should assume that *all* employees have a healthy sense of commitment to getting the job done to the best of their ability, unless proven otherwise. Simultaneously, you should be prepared if a colleague shows a lack of commitment. Being committed (or not committed) is ultimately a personal choice. But you can influence commitment levels somewhat. There's no better vehicle than having an encouragement conversation.

How do you extract commitment from an employee in a conversation? Ask. Ask the employee for their commitment. Ask them to commit to achieving a quality outcome. *Can I get your commitment to achieve this result?* If the team member in the conversation verbalizes their commitment, you can hold them accountable for that. If they aren't willing to commit, this signifies the beginning of an entirely different kind of conversation! Managers can often assume they have employee's commitment, and don't bother asking for it. By not asking, the team member hasn't made a verbal commitment—and that's part of the problem.

Friendship

One of the most underrated retention and engagement factors is the camaraderie and friendships made at work. Although you can't directly influence who is friends with whom, people do form friendships at work. But you can encourage and promote positive social interaction. And as we know, friendships are developed through conversation.

The encouraging conversation does enable the development of higher levels of trust and camaraderie between you and your colleagues. But regrettably, mistrust and antagonism are the norm in many workplaces. Worse still, I've witnessed—as I'm sure you have—managers using 'divide and rule' tactics; that is, creating divisions between people as a means of maintaining control. This is discouraging and disengaging, to say the least.

Progress

Conversations on the progress of work tasks is natural. But conversations on the progress of people's development isn't routine—and that's disappointing. Talking to team members about their progress or—more particularly—their lack of progress can be heartening, if done with care. The performance conversations in Part III cover progress in greater detail. I suggest five more conversations I refer to as the *Five Conversations Framework*, that help a person grow and develop personally and technically.

Regular conversations on personal progress are often uplifting. *How have you settled in? Where do you think you are making progress or inroads in your job? What's challenging you now with your work?* These questions are a springboard for discussing headway.

Discussing progress also shows interest in the welfare of the person. And it helps to gauge how the person is feeling about their job. Progress conversations don't need to be long. These conversations can take place in a matter of minutes in the corridor, when the opportunity arises.

As an update, encouragement can come from:

- clarifying expectations,
- looking after working conditions,
- building upon the strengths,
- acknowledging good work,
- respecting the person doing the job,

- inviting their views and opinions where appropriate,
- explaining the relevance of the work they do,
- gaining their commitment,
- building friendships, and
- discussing progress.

Learning and Growing

I explicitly cover the learning and development conversation in Chap. 22. Encouragement can come from discussing growth opportunities. People can be inspired by their involvement in a challenging work assignment or project, for instance. This might entail applying some well-known job redesign strategies such as *job rotation*, *job enrichment*, *job enlargement*, or *multi-skilling*.[1]

Giving someone an opportunity to swap jobs with someone else for a set period is a growth opportunity. This is what's commonly referred to as job rotation. Job enrichment can involve delegating a demanding one-off assignment or project to build a team member's skills-set. Job enlargement is slightly different—it involves giving extra responsibilities to a team member for a finite period. This could be taking on supervisory responsibilities while the leader is away, for example. Multi-skilling comprises the opportunity to learn and sample new skills beyond the scope of a team member's current job description. Often, multi-skilling is done in a structured way involving everyone in the team. These well-established development opportunities, when applied properly, can stimulate engagement and human spirit.

Discussing these prospects helps employees stretch beyond their current capabilities. Someone with reasonable self-confidence and a growth mindset will relish these opportunities—with a bit of encouragement from you. A conversation about this signifies to the team member that you have faith in their ability to take on more responsibility—they are likely to be reassured, if nothing else.

An affirmative response for each of Gallup Corporation's Q12 engagement survey questions would suggest that the person has a high level of engagement. The encouraging conversation is a great vehicle to discuss these 12 themes—not necessarily all in the one conversation! This conversation is essentially about positive feedback, emphasizing effort and improvement. Encouragement is not the same as praise. Although praise is a part of encouragement. But praise is generally given by a leader when tangible achievements have been accomplished. Encouragement, on the other hand, is generally about the means and progress made toward an outcome.

For example, consider Q7: *At work, do your opinions seem to count?* For an employee to be able to answer positively, they need to be encouraged to speak up, in a non-threatening way. Getting others to offer their opinions is done by asking them for their opinions. And then to actively and patiently listening with interest to the person's perspective. These attributes demonstrate respect, appreciation, and a caring attitude. It's encouraging.

In summary, the 12 items open for discussion in an encouraging conversation are:

- clarifying expectations,
- making sure employees have the right tools for the job,
- utilizing the innate talents of the employee,
- providing regular recognition and acknowledgement of good work,
- respecting workers as people first and foremost,
- supporting their development,
- taking an interest in their opinions,
- clarifying the relevance of the work tasks,
- asking for their commitment,
- building social connections,
- reviewing progress, and
- providing growth opportunities.

This brings us to the end of the chapter. In the final two chapters in Part II, we consider the relationship building conversation.

The Top 10 Key Points …

1. One of the core responsibilities of any leader is to set and communicate their expectations to their team.
2. To achieve optimal performance and be fully engaged, employees need the right resources to do the job they are employed to do.
3. Employees should be given the opportunity to do what they do best every day.
4. Organizational psychologists keep tell us that most people need positive reinforcement and encouragement to flourish at work.
5. Support a team member in their personal and technical development is another important element of leadership.

6. Displaying commitment to do quality work is characteristic of an engaged employee.
7. People like it when they know their opinions count for something.
8. One of the most underrated retention and engagement factors is the camaraderie and friendships made at work.
9. The encouraging conversation based on discussing progress shows interest in the welfare of the person.
10. Discussing developmental opportunities encourages the team member to stretch themselves beyond their current capabilities.

Note

1. https://study.com/academy/lesson/types-of-job-redesign-job-enrichment-enlargement-rotation.html.

15

Conversation 5: The Relationship Building Conversation

> *Listening isn't just a transaction or exchange of words, but a relational connection that involves and affects the mind, the body, and the heart.*

Can you imagine a work situation where two people sit side-by-side for 10 years without uttering one word to each other; not even a hello, good morning, how are you? Not one word! Well, it happened!

I worked with an internationally recognized orchestra. Two musicians sit next to each other on the stage and in rehearsal. They refused to speak to one another for a decade. When they had to communicate with each other about artistic matters, they would write notes and pass them to each other without making eye contact.

After sitting down with each of the musicians separately in a coaching session, I was told of a relatively minor incident that occurred between these two artists early in their career in the orchestra. Although a trivial matter on the surface, it resulted in a major violation of trust and they both decided not to speak to each other for what amounted to thousands of rehearsals, orchestral meetings, and concerts. It created tension in their section and ultimately across the entire orchestra. The section principal musician didn't know what to do and eventually gave up trying to reconcile their differences.

I suggested to both musicians separately to meet over coffee and reconcile their differences and talk together. I arranged the meeting. And they did finally, reluctantly meet. Their differences were ironed out and now they are happily communicating again.[1]

Relationships are important, even in the workplace. If people have healthy working relationships it underwrites an environment conducive to stimulating human spirit at work. The opposite is true too: poor working relationships can make work unattractive. Robust working relationships—particularly between managers and team members—can inspire and motivate. More trust amounts to added self-assurance. Additionally, the leader is eager to encourage development and mastery with those they have a healthy working relationship with. People are on the same page; they are clear about their purpose and direction. Dignity is present. The five pillars of authenticity are characteristic of their conversations.

I frequently discuss feedback with managers. When people hear the word *feedback* they instinctively think of criticism—even though praise, acknowledgement, and recognition are also forms of feedback. And therefore, my discussion with managers often moves to looking for opportunities to give positive feedback—partly to reset the tendency to assume feedback is inevitably critical or negative.

One line that helps to grasp the significance of sharing positive feedback is this: *If the only time I hear from you is when you think I've screwed up, what do you think that relationship is going to be like?* It's not difficult to imagine the quality of a relationship if the only feedback an employee receives is negative. Your relationship with your boss—who is constantly negative—will be one of avoiding interaction, not taking risks, being prepared to defend myself, and to see them as a threat rather than a supporter, more than likely. From the manager's perspective, their relationship with you will be shaped by their experiences of your defensiveness and lack of initiative. Neither you nor your boss is probably going to look forward to your next interaction. You both aren't going to share positive messages about each other with your extended networks. Neither of you will experience a sense of teamwork and harmony when together. This is hardly surprising, since the experience each of you have of your conversations is characterized by criticism, defensiveness, authority, resistance, frustration, and resentment. Negative feedback—with no positive feedback—erodes any working relationship.

Now consider how this relationship dynamic might change. Your boss decides to take the initiative to express appreciation for something you've done. Perhaps they shared a positive comment someone else had made about your work. Or your manager took a few minutes to ask you how things were going? If your relationship hasn't been great then it will take more than one interaction to recalibrate it, but it's a constructive start. And all it takes mostly is a few of those types of genuine conversations to begin to reset the connection between the two of you.

Let's look at some of the dynamics at play in conversations. What are the principles and practices you can employ to use our interactions as opportunities to build healthier relationships that enable more robust and honest conversations.

Relationships and Tasks

Most of our workplace interaction tends to be task-specific. I talked about this in Chap. 3 in some detail. By task-specific, I'm referring to discussing goals, projects, processes, plans, actions, responses, and results. And that's appropriate, because teams need to be able to perform, achieve, and deliver. The hazard, however, is that we miss the fact that sustainable performance of those tasks is directly affected by the relationships between those working on the tasks. Indeed, conflict in teams typically occurs over task issues, relationship issues, or process issues—including the processes used to resolve task and relationship issues.

An analysis of 45 independent studies of team conflict (involving more than 3000 teams) found that

> conflict processes, that is, how teams *interact regarding* their differences, are at least as important as conflict states, that is, the *source* and *intensity* of those perceived differences.[2]

Unsurprisingly, Leslie DeChurch and her colleagues found that what they called "collectivist processes" (such as openness and collaboration) produced better team outcomes than "individualistic processes" (such as competing or avoiding).[3] What seems like commonsense, though, is challenging—because individuals and teams often simply don't know how to engage in open and collaborative processes, especially during conflict.

What this suggests is that an intentional focus on conversations that build relationships is not an end in itself. Rather, it's a practical means of ensuring that teams not only focus on and achieve their tasks, but also support one another. It's the relationships within the team that enable tasks to be managed and achieved in cooperative, creative, and sustainable ways.

This brings us back to the central role of conversations—the conversations individuals have with each other and the conversations teams have—and the principles and practices that shape and empower those conversations. Let's look at some of these principles.

Trust

There's no doubting the significance of trust—whether we are talking about relationships between people, between individuals and their leaders, or between people and their organizations. *Edelman PR* have been tracking trust in government and business around the world for many years, each year releasing a "trust barometer":

> We believe trust is an asset that enterprises must understand and properly manage in order to be successful in today's complex operating environment. Unlike reputation, which is based on an aggregate of past experiences with a company or brand, trust is a forward-facing metric of stakeholder expectation.[4]

In his book, *The Speed of Trust*, Stephen M.R. Covey makes the case for investing in trust relationships with his equation that when trust goes up, speed goes up and cost goes down, and when trust goes down, speed goes down and cost goes up.[5] Or, as Ralph Waldo Emerson put it: "Our distrust is very expensive." Trust or distrust is something that facilitates or hinders individual, team, and organizational performance.

So how do we build trust? In short, the answer is, one conversation at a time.

There are numerous descriptions of trust, but some of the commonly agreed features include:

1. openness,
2. acceptance,
3. congruence (alignment between what we say and what we mean),
4. reliability, and
5. competence.

These are experienced, communicated, and assessed through our conversations—both those we are a part of and those we observe. So, let's take a quick surf through these five elements of trust.

1. *Openness*

The level of openness we offer others in conversations gives the other person a sense of our self-confidence and willingness to connect with them. We talk about some people being 'closed books' or 'playing their cards close to their chest'—suggesting it's hard for us to know what they're really like. Trust requires a degree of openness or self-disclosure about ourselves.

Being open can be risky. But trust is about building safety and elevating understanding, so we can accomplish more together in the face of risk. Some people are more naturally open about themselves than others (which is not always a good thing—especially if you're seated next to them on a long flight!). But any healthy relationship needs a commitment to exchange information and appropriately self-disclosing to communicate faithfulness to the relationship. We can't realistically expect others to give us information and let us know about themselves if we aren't willing to do the same. That means leaders ought to take the first step in being open.

2. *Acceptance*

Acceptance is the flipside of the openness coin. When people do share information about themselves they've chosen to take a risk—to be a little bit vulnerable. We know there's a chance of rejection or negative judgment. It's important therefore that we manage our prejudices and biases. We need to accept others for who they are and acknowledge their perspectives as their own—even if we don't agree. It's not always easy, but it is important.

3. *Congruence*

Congruence in the context of communication is measured by the association of our words with their meaning. Do we talk straight? Or do we couch our opinions and contributions in qualifications or hesitant phrases? There's a balance, of course, between bluntness and evasion. We tend to trust 'straight shooters' over obfuscators. But being blunt has its limitations.

At any rate, the language people use is usually a lot stronger than the actions they're prepared to take. Congruence is about being assertive. It's the equilibrium between aggressiveness and avoidance. Trust and congruence go together. Congruence communicates respect—respect for our views and respect for the capacity of others to handle our directness.

4. *Reliability*

Reliability is the most familiar element of trust. At its core, reliability sends a message about whether you will *do what you say you will do*. Over-promising, under-delivering, procrastinating, and inconsistency are traits of being unreliable. And being unreliable means being untrustworthy.

5. *Competence*

Competence is a fifth element of trust—often associated with reliability—that is sometimes overlooked. We learn to trust ourselves and others in some situations, but not others. We may trust our own judgment in financial matters, based on our expertise in that area. But we may not trust ourselves to make a hiring decision because we acknowledge our limitations there, perhaps based on an unfortunate experience. Likewise, we may trust our manager to competently organize a project, but not to make a presentation about it to stakeholders. Our trust is largely dependent upon the task competence of the person we are interacting with. Since our physical, emotional, and professional safety is fundamental to us, we instinctively look for demonstrated competence. Competence is part of our trust assessment.

Each of the five elements of trust: openness, acceptance, congruence, reliability, and competence are integral in relationship building. And so, it's important we consciously remember these elements in our conversations.

> **Where the Rubber Meets the Road …**
>
> **Growing Trust in your Work Relationships**
>
> Relationships that enable trust and bring exceptional results don't happen unless there's a conscious intention to make them happen. That intention starts with common-sense approaches around *basic* relationship building. Below are 10 ways to demonstrate that a work relationship matters.
> Trust grows in relationships when …
> The relationships are mutually beneficial.
> You bring the best of who you are into the relationship; the best includes core elements like integrity, tolerance, honesty, and trustworthiness.
> You want the best for the other person.
> The relationship is more important than any single outcome.
> You invest time, communication, commitment, and authenticity.
> You show genuine care, concern, and compassion.
> You operate with appreciation, politeness, and inclusion.
> You give more than you take, while keeping your interests in view.
> You help others achieve their aspirations, dreams, goals, or personal best.
> You respect where others are coming from—knowledge, experience, state of mind, values, beliefs, needs.
> Trust—particularly in governments[6]—may be at historic lows, but so what? Trust is a local issue. If you want more trust in your work relationships, start with yourself. A practice of trust building is a practice of relationship building. If you want to grow trust or rebuild broken trust, focus on building your relationships.[7]

Openness, Appreciation, and Interest

Elsewhere in this book, I have covered several important, but often neglected positive conversations—conversations that focus on what's working well, what we appreciate, what we are grateful for (see Chap. 13—The Encouraging Conversation and Chap. 20—The Strengths and Talents Conversation). Such conversations are a natural means of expressing openness and acceptance as part of the trust building process. They're also energizing for both the recipient and the person delivering the positive messages.

My colleague, Aubrey Warren, and co-author of *Conversations at Work* recalls a wise summer camp director's mantra to his staff that every teenage camper should receive "a measure of challenge, a measure of achievement, and a measure of recognition every day."[8] It's a practical aspiration that reminds us of the importance of respecting those we have the privilege of leading.

Goffee and Jones call it the need for *significance*.

> Followers need to feel significant. In simple terms, they need recognition for their contribution. Social psychologists have made repeated pronouncements on this profound human need for recognition. So it is remarkable how often as individuals we seem to want it but not give it.[9]

Showing interest in others, expressing appreciation for efforts, and giving recognition for achievements and contributions are simple but powerful conversations to have. These conversations invest in relationships and building confidence and trust. They include the coaching conversation (see Chap. 7) and the encouraging conversation (see Chap. 13). In Part III, the most obvious performance conversation to expresses appreciation is the strengths and talents conversation (see Chap. 20).

Empathetic Listening

"The ability and willingness to listen with empathy is often what sets a leader apart," says Christine Riordan, professor of management at the University of Kentucky.

> Hearing words is not adequate; the leader truly needs to work at understanding the position and perspective of the others involved in the conversation.[10]

Riordan urges leaders to focus on three skills to escalate empathetic listening:

- observing nonverbal cues,
- processing information attentively and checking for understanding, and
- encouraging the conversation to continue through verbal and nonverbal acknowledgements.

These skills reinforce the message that listening isn't just a transaction or exchange of words, but a relational connection that involves and affects the mind, the body, and the heart. And it's the heart aspect—the *pathos*—that human beings naturally remember most vividly. Remember the old saying that *no one cares how much you know until they know how much you care*.

In the final chapter of Part II, we consider five steps to better relationship building conversations.

The Top 10 Key Points …

1. Relationships are important, even in the workplace. If people have healthy working relationships it underwrites an environment conducive to stimulating human spirit at work.
2. An intentional focus on conversations that build relationships is not an end in itself.
3. There's no doubting the significance of trust—whether we are talking about relationships between people, between individuals and their leaders, or between people and their organizations.
4. There are numerous descriptions of trust, but some of the commonly agreed elements of trust are openness, acceptance, congruence (alignment between what we say and what we mean), reliability, and competence.
5. The level of openness we offer others in conversations gives the other person a sense of our self-confidence and willingness to connect with them.
6. Acceptance is the flipside of the openness coin. When people do share information about themselves they've chosen to take a risk—to be a little bit vulnerable.
7. Congruence in the context of communication is measured by the association of our words with their meaning.
8. Reliability is the most familiar element of trust. At its core, reliability sends a message about whether you will do what you say you will do.
9. Competence—often associated with reliability—that is sometimes overlooked. We learn to trust ourselves and others in some situations, but not others.
10. Showing interest in others, expressing appreciation for efforts, and giving recognition for achievements and contributions are simple but powerful conversations to have.

Notes

1. Baker, T.B. & Warren, A. (2015). Conversations at work: Promoting a culture of conversation in the changing workplace. London: Palgrave Macmillan.
2. DeChurch, L.A., Mesmer-Magnus, J.R., & Doty, D. (2013). Moving beyond relationship and task conflict: Toward a process-state perspective. *Journal of Applied Psychology*, 98, 4, 559–578.
3. Ibid.
4. Edelman (2014). 2014 Edelman trust barometer. http://www.edelman.com.
5. Covey, S.M.R., & Merrill, R.R. (2006). The speed of trust: The one thing that changes everything. New York: Free Press.
6. Edelman (2014). 2014 Edelman trust barometer. http://www.edelman.com.
7. http://www.psychologytoday.com/blog/trust-the-new-workplace-currency/201309/ten-ways-cultivate-work-relationships-and-grow-trust.
8. Baker, T.B. & Warren, A. (2015). Conversations at work: Promoting a conversation culture in a changing workplace. London: Palgrave Macmillan.
9. Goffee, R. & Jones, G. (2006). Why should anyone be led by you? Boston, MA: Harvard Business School Press.
10. Riordan, C.M. (2014). Three ways leaders can listen with more empathy. http://blogs.hbr.org/2014/01/three-ways-leaders-can-listen-with-more-empathy/.

16

Five Steps to Relationship Building Conversations

When someone does display the nerve and skill to speak up candidly, respectfully, and confidently about the real issue, everyone sits up straighter and recognizes that something important has happened. This is authenticity-in-action.

In this final chapter of Part II, we consider five important steps needed to build better relationships. In our book *Conversations at Work*, Aubrey Warren and I outline four steps to relationship building conversations. I've added a fifth step in this chapter.

There's a lot going on in a conversation. It's more than the words spoken and heard. It's more than the non-verbal communication accompanying the conversation. It's more than the interpretation of the message. It's the combination of these components and more that shapes the relationship between conversation partners. One way to think about effectively managing your conversations is through five practices that can be applied to build relationships:

- Step 1: Show up;
- Step 2: Listen up;
- Step 3: Speak up;
- Step 4: Lift up; and
- Step 5: Follow up

I'll walk you through these steps in the next few pages.

Step 1: Show Up

Showing up means being present in the conversation. This sounds easy. But we know how it feels when the person we are trying to communicate with isn't present. They might be checking their phone or looking over our shoulder, or just has that slightly glazed look that silently but powerfully says, *are you done yet?* Managing our attention is harder to practice in our increasingly frantic lives than it may seem. But since we can't physically be anywhere other than where we are, it makes sense to show up 100 per cent. We'll get more out of the exchange and our conversation partners will contribute more, knowing we are fully engaged.

One of the paradoxes of leadership conversations is being in the moment and simultaneously having peripheral vision. Leaders need the capacity to listen at two levels. At one level they need to be present and at another level, they need to consider a host of factors away from the dialog that affect the current conversation. There's a difference, however, between sustaining these two levels of listening and showing up. Typing out an email while listening to an employee isn't peripheral vision. It's often justified as multitasking. Showing up means giving the other person your full attention.

Adam Fraser in his book, *The 3rd Space*, contends that one of the great challenges we face is the task of dealing with the constant 'transitions' between the many tasks and settings we work in every day:

The key to business success is the ability to leave the mindset and baggage of the previous interaction behind and psychologically 'show up' to the next one with a mindset that will get the most out of it.[1]

One of Fraser's practical tips is to anticipate the new interaction and ask ourselves how we want to show up—and then behave in that way. Without consciously redirecting our behaviors, our attention, and our thinking to the other person and the issue-at-hand, there's every likelihood we'll behave inappropriately and ineffectively. How we show up is how people experience us. So, how do you want to show up? How do others need you to show up? How will the way you show up enrich the conversation and the relationship?

Step 2: Listen Up

I've mentioned the importance of listening several times so far and will do so again before the finish. Why? It's critically important. Listening is foundational to our success as communicators, leaders, and influencers. And it's central to showing up and being fully present. "The biggest mistake you can make in trying to talk convincingly is to put your highest priority on expressing your ideas and feelings," wrote John Maxwell in *Developing the Leader Within You*.

What most people really want is to be listened to, respected and understood. The moment people see that they are being understood they become motivated to understand your point of view.[2]

The challenges of really listening are many—not least the fact that your brain's capacity to process information runs about four times the rate at which you speak. And its difficulty is further compounded by our tendency to assume we know where the person is going with their thoughts, rather than focusing on and processing what they're saying. This means we can easily find ourselves listening more actively to our own thoughts and judgments about the other person than to what they're saying. For many of us, these two practical challenges are supplemented by the inability to focus—because we suffer from 'monkey mind.'

Monkey mind is a term from Buddhism. It describes the untrained mind as being restless and easily distracted, jumping chaotically from one idea to another like a monkey in a tree. It's our internal dialog that mentally interrupts, distracts, and distorts the moments and conversations we're in.

Step 3: Speak Up

Speaking up may seem an obvious component in healthy conversations. But everyone knows the frustration, uncertainty, and anxiety that's created when important issues are left unspoken. We talk about not mentioning the 'elephant in the room.' Lots of words are spoken, but no one has the courage to speak up about what really matters. But when someone does display the nerve and skill to speak up candidly, respectfully, and confidently about the real issue, everyone sits up straighter and recognizes that something important has happened. This is authenticity-in-action.

That is a premise of the bestselling *Crucial Conversations*.

Research has shown that strong relationships, careers, organizations, and communities all draw from the same source of power—the ability to talk openly about high-stakes, emotional, controversial topics.[3]

The ability to speak up in highly charged situations doesn't usually happen spontaneously or accidentally. It's borne out of the experience of speaking up honestly, clearly, and respectfully in lots of everyday, ordinary conversations.

Showing up, listening up, and speaking up are all essential factors in relationship building conversations. But there's two additional elements that we frequently overlook, although they are usually well within our reach. They are the two ingredients that can put your conversations on relationship steroids.

Step 4: Lift Up

Lifting up is the conscious commitment to leave the conversation with people feeling positive. This sounds like a great idea, but … what about when you have no choice but to criticize, correct, or insist on compliance? What about when the exchange has been terse, tough, or filled with tension? Perhaps in such instances it's even more important to aim to *lift up*—not just the other person—but yourself too.

How? Not with the old 'feedback sandwich' (positive opening … critical message … positive close). We all know to listen for that middle bit and ignore the rest. We can, however, keep a couple of principles in mind that can help ensure even those difficult conversations conclude on an upward note.

You've probably noted the tendency for conversations to follow one of two directions—up or down. This is sometimes called the 'upward spiral' or 'downward spiral' of a conversation. In a downward spiral, you hear the language and tone becoming negative, strained, tired, and de-energized. Conversely, in upward spiral conversations the language and tone maintain or even build energy. This is achieved through positive framing of messages, solution-focused debate, respectful listening, and a sense of shared purpose. As a leader, it's important to take responsibility to deliberately influence this spiral—directing the spiral up and intervening if it heads south.

Some conversations will inevitably head down naturally as you get into the detail of a difficult issue. That's okay. But if you're going to work toward a solution or constructive outcome, you need to shape a positive mindset. There's a point at which the downward problem focus needs to be transitioned into a future, solution focus. Remember, I discussed this as one of the pillars of authentic conversation in Chap. 6. This is the idea of creating 'shared meaning' and 'co-creating' our conversations. Keeping a clear emphasis on what the issue is and what we're trying to achieve gives a strong impetus to building and preserving an upward spiral.

This spiral—upward or downward—is molded from the first words we utter in a conversation. The principle of 'primacy and recency' has a significant effect on conversations. The beginning and ending of a conversation will, in other words, have a heavier weighting on our recollection of our experience of conversation than the actual content. This again reinforces that how we show up (see 'showing up' above) sets the tone and likely direction of a conversation. How we close will also leave a lasting impression of the time and effort we've invested in the conversation. Therefore, ensuring that your conversations conclude with clear commitments—to action, to the next step, to further conversation—is important. You should strive to leave your conversation partner (and yourself) with a sense of value, purpose, and progress from the interaction.

Clear-cut commitments can include shared decision-making, comprehensible direction, succinct summaries, or explicit next steps. It's easy for two people to leave the same conversation with different conclusions. We've all experienced this. So, clarifying and confirming your shared understanding and commitments helps you and your conversation partner to build positive energy in the conversation and ultimately, the relationship.

Having led with an upward spiral and concluded with a common understanding, you're in a good position to add one final touch—affirmation. Even when you have 'agreed to disagree' or simply settled that you have competing commitments, there's nothing (apart from overactive emotions) that prevents you from acknowledging the other party's contribution to the conversation. Say thank you, acknowledge their contribution, appreciate their perspective, or express gratitude for their candor. Any of these affirmations leave the other person feeling respected and valued. Affirming is a simple act, but one that will make an indelible investment to the working relationship as well as to how the issue is managed.

> **Where the Rubber Meets the Road ...**
> **Use Conversations to Start Virtual Team Meetings**
> Keith Ferrazzi, CEO of *Ferrazzi Greenlight*, in the Harvard Business Review article: *Getting virtual teams right* gave this helpful tip for virtual teams: While employees who are in the same office commonly chat about their lives, virtual teammates do so much more rarely. Try taking five minutes at the beginning of conference calls for everyone to share a recent professional success or some personal news. This is probably the easiest way to overcome the isolation that can creep in when people don't work together physically.[4]

Step 5: Follow Up

Aubrey Warren added another step after we launched our book, *Conversations at Work*. This was *Follow up*.

Following up matters. It makes a difference. Follow up sends at least three important messages to the people we lead. First, it signals that what you're doing counts. It matters that you get that project finished on time. It matters to adopt that new process. It matters to expand your network. It matters to establish a new client relationship. It matters to gather the necessary information to make an informed decision. There is a familiar adage that *what gets followed up, gets done.*

Second, following up says that your success has a bearing. One of Aubrey Warren's favorite leadership maxims is that 'leadership is about creating the conditions for success.' Leaders invest in the development of others. They want to see the people they work with succeed. Follow up is a tangible expression of this focus on success. Follow up reinforces the significance of what people are doing—it highlights that it matters, and that it has value.

Third, it says that you matter. Following up lets the people know you care about them, as well as what they are doing. It acknowledges their significance. Follow up communicates attention. It meets a basic human need to feel valued and be acknowledged. Treating people as numbers or anonymous entities doesn't invite creative contribution. It seems our workplaces still by-and-large see—and treat—people as cogs in the machine, as we discussed in Part I. And there's only so much you can achieve with a cog. Capturing creativity, sparking initiative, and boosting discretionary effort means harnessing human capacity. For these qualities to be unleashed, an environment that respects, values, and celebrates humanity is necessary. How do your people know they matter? How do they experience it? What enables them to believe it?[5]

In this chapter, we have covered five key steps in building relationships. They include show up, listen up, speak up, lift up, and follow up. In the previous chapter, we looked at trust, recognition, appreciation, interest, and empathetic listening. Like the other four conversations in Part II, you can now go out and practice it.

This brings us to the end of Part II. Part II covered five developmental conversations that are important to any leader. They are developmental because they are people-focused conversations. These five conversations are about developing the person and your relationship with that person. We covered the coaching, delegation, visioning, encouraging, and relationship building conversation.

In Part III, the focus changes slightly. We consider performance conversations. The five conversations I refer to in Part III are part of a framework. I call this the Five Conversations Framework. The theme is performance development.

The Top 10 Key Points …

1. The five practices for building relationships are show up, listen up, speak up, lift up, and follow up.
2. Showing up means being present in the conversation.

3. One of the paradoxes of leadership conversations is being in the moment and simultaneously having peripheral vision.
4. Listening is foundational to our effectiveness as communicators, leaders, and influencers.
5. The challenges of really listening are many—not least the fact that your brain's capacity to process information runs about four times the rate at which you speak.
6. Speaking up may seem an obvious component in healthy conversations. But everyone knows the frustration, uncertainty, and anxiety that's created when important issues are left unspoken.
7. The ability to speak up in those highly charged situations doesn't happen spontaneously or accidentally.
8. Lifting up is the conscious commitment to leave the conversation with people feeling positive.
9. You've probably noted the tendency for conversations to follow one of two directions—up or down. This is sometimes called the 'upward spiral' or 'downward spiral' of a conversation.
10. Follow up does three important things: It says what matters; that your success counts; and that the other person matter too.

Notes

1. Fraser, A. (2012). *The 3rd space: How to show up with the right mindset every time*. http://dradamfraser.com/about/services/keynote-speaking/the-3rd-space-managing-how-you-show-up.html#.VCDp2U0cSP8.
2. Maxwell, J. (1993) Developing the leader within you. Thomas Nelson.
3. Patterson, K., Grenny, J., McMillan, R., & Switzler, A. (2012). Crucial conversations: Tools for talking when the stakes are high (2nd Ed.). McGraw-Hill.
4. Ferrazzi, K. (2014). Getting virtual teams right. *Harvard Business Review* (December). https://hbr.org/2014/12/getting-virtual-teams-right#signin.
5. This material on Follow up has been paraphrased from an article in one of Aubrey Warren's recent newsletters to his clients.

Part III

Five Performance Conversations

17

Overview of the Five Conversations Framework

Outstanding leaders ... build professional rapport and understanding with their team members by having regular conversations about performance and development (people-focused conversations).

It's 9 am on Monday and Bob is sitting across the desk in Terry's large office. The early morning sun is streaming through the half-closed louvers and casting some shadows across Terry's big, black shiny desk. It's annual performance review time and everyone is on their best behavior. There is an understandable degree of tension and apprehension around the office. Sitting in the chair opposite Terry, Bob looks as though he's sitting in an airport lounge, having just been told that his flight has been delayed an hour and it's already 10.30 at night.

Terry—Bob's boss—isn't feeling his best either. He's a little anxious about appraising Bob's performance. As Terry is reading through Bob's self-appraisal behind his large, imposing desk, Bob sits with a look of disinterest on his face, chewing a piece of gum, arms folded, and staring straight ahead into the distance.

With some variation, this familiar scene is being played out in almost every office, production area, and worksite at the time of the annual performance review. So familiar are we with this scene, the UK BBC sitcom *The Office* has a hilarious parody on the annual appraisal. The skit shows 'David' conducting the annual performance appraisal on 'Keith' in David's office. This scene is readily available through *YouTube*—check it out if you have not already seen it, it's entertaining. But like most good comedy, it has more than a glimmer of truth to it.

In that skit, David struggles his way through myriad paperwork. Keith is completely detached, arms folded, deadpan expression, and less than helpful on the other side of the desk. David asks Keith why he hasn't completed the self-appraisal form, and Keith responds by saying he thought David was supposed to fill this in as his boss. It goes downhill from there.

In obvious frustration, David moves on to the 'Q and A' section of the appraisal paperwork. Again, this isn't completed. David uses this as an opportunity to engage Keith. "To what extent have you been trained to use the computer effectively?" David reads from the forms, without making eye contact. With no reply from Keith, David recites the suite of options: "One, not at all; two, to some extent; three, reasonably competent; four, competent; five, very competent; or don't know." "Don't know," comes the unconsidered reply from Keith, still staring into space.

Plowing on, "To what extent do you feel you are given the freedom and support to accomplish your goals?" "What are the options again?" asks Keith. "Always the same. One, not at all; two, to some extent; three, reasonably competent; four, competent; five, very competent; or don't know." "Don't know" comes the humdrum reply from Keith again. And on it goes in the same non-communicative and painful patter.

In the end, David challenges Keith by asking, "If 'don't know' wasn't an option, what would you put?" To which Keith replies, "What was the question again?"

Somewhat exaggerated perhaps, but nevertheless this is the kind of disengagement that happens across all industries for a high percentage of employees and managers once or twice a year.

I'm sure you have your own war stories, either as someone like David conducting the appraisal or like Keith, the person on the receiving end of the appraisal, or both.

The Five Conversations Framework focuses on individual and organizational performance. It looks at five dimensions of performance and is based on the concept of human spirit and work I covered in Chap. 2. Participants in these conversations—as distinct from the five developmental conversations covered in Part II—should come to the dialog prepared to enrich the conversation. All five conversations in the framework are based on helping the team member to build upon their strengths and minimize their areas of weakness. These conversations—like the previous five developmental conversations—are supposed to be elevating and are consistent with the five pillars of authentic conversations we covered in Chaps. 5 and 6.

It offers a fresh approach to managing performance, based on regular conversations. The framework is designed to replace the traditional once-a-year performance review. However, the five conversations themselves can be useful—regardless of whether you have a performance review system in place or not. This chapter gives you an overview of the framework. The subsequent five chapters in Part III cover each conversation in some detail.

In a nutshell, the Five Conversations Framework is based on five conversations between the leader and team member. The conversations take place once a month over a five-month period. Each of the conversations need only last 20 minutes or so. Over the course of a year, using this new system, I encourage managers to have 10 conversations with each of their colleagues. In other words, each conversation occurs twice a year.

The conversations are based on themes or topics, like the five conversations we covered in Part II. These conversations are designed to be less formal, more relaxed, more frequent, and more focused than the conventional once- or twice-a-year performance review.

Although the framework is new, there isn't anything novel about the idea of sitting down and discussing performance with employees, despite it not happening as often as it ought to. This frequent, less formal, and more focused dialog should be something that managers participate in with their colleagues anyway. Outstanding leaders in my experience build professional rapport and understanding with their team members by having regular performance and development conversations. (people-focused conversations).

The Five Conversations Framework is based on performance. Although it should be par for the course, regular constructive conversations about performance rarely take place in most workplaces.

Some managers pull up their direct reports when things aren't done properly. But sub-standard work is only one dimension of performance—as important as it is. What's more, managers have regular conversations about task-focused matters, as we've discussed. But rarely do they engage in a two-way dialog about other dimensions of performance beyond mistakes or routine tasks. And when other performance dimensions are raised, they usually occur during the appraisal interview. In these forums, they're usually done formally and in a perfunctory manner. As such, they are an appraisal of performance rather than a discussion on how performance can be improved.

So, what are these other dimensions of performance? And how does the framework help?

Table 17.1 illustrates the suggested frequency, topics, and content. This table forms the framework for the five conversations we cover in Part III.

The first conversation—climate review—is based on job satisfaction, morale, and communication. Conversation number two—strengths and talents—is concerned with identifying strengths and capabilities and how best they may be

Table 17.1 The five conversations framework

Date	Theme	Content
Month 1	Climate review	Job satisfaction, morale, and communications
Month 2	Strengths and talents	The effective use of strengths and innate talents now and in the future
Month 3	Opportunities for growth	Improving areas of performance on the job
Month 4	Learning and development	Growth opportunity and support
Month 5	Innovation and continuous improvement	Improving the efficiency and effectiveness of the workplace

used for the benefit of team member and the team. The third conversation discusses opportunities for growth. This conversation is essentially about recognizing and filling gaps in performance. Building on the two previous conversations, it's timely to consider learning and development opportunities. The learning and development conversation is concerned with ways and means of building upon the team member's strengths and minimizing their weaknesses. Innovation and continuous improvement, the fifth and final conversation discusses ideas to improve the efficiency and effectiveness of the business.

Each of the five conversations has a distinct focus, building upon the previous discussion. Together, the framework adopts a multidimensional approach to performance. There is a logic to the order of these conversations. This framework is based upon the following flow of questions:

1. How satisfied are you in your current job and what do you observe about team morale and communication? (Climate review)
2. What are your strengths and talents and how can they be best exercised in your current and possible future roles in the organization? (Strengths and talents)
3. What are some opportunities for growth in your current and possible future roles in the organization? (Opportunities for growth)
4. How can you capitalize on your strengths and build your opportunities for growth? (Learning and development)
5. What suggestions can you make to improve your work environment? (Innovation and continuous improvement)

Each of these core questions supporting the five conversations uses information from the previous conversations and builds upon it.

Here is an illustration for you to see the process in action.

Let's assume that Harry has indicated to his manager, Claire—during the climate review conversation—that he's currently experiencing low job satisfaction (a rating of 3 out of 10). When asked why his rating is so low, Harry tells Claire that he's not suited to his current position—he feels his capabilities are not being fully utilized.

In their second conversation (strengths and talents) a month later, Harry states that he thinks he's more analytical and that the sales role he currently has is not suited to this strength. They both agree that Harry's role should have less emphasis on selling and more on analyzing the sales activities of the 10 salespeople in the team. This analysis would help Claire to better understand the nature of sales activity in the team and provide useful data on customer feedback for future planning.

In the opportunities for growth conversation one month later, Harry acknowledges that he has never undergone any formal training on data analysis. This is despite having an obvious aptitude for analysis.

In the fourth conversation (learning and development), Harry and Claire identify a course of study that will assist Harry in gaining the necessary theoretical knowledge and skills to undertake his new role.

And finally, in the innovation and continuous improvement conversation, with Claire's prompting, Harry suggests an incentive program be implemented to encourage salespeople to record information from their sales visits. These data could then be used by Harry in his analysis of customer feedback. Claire likes Harry's idea.

These five conversations lead to a productive outcome for Harry, Claire, and the organization.

Benefits of the Five Conversations Framework

Imagine for a moment how powerful this process could be if implemented across an entire organization, that is, everyone is engaged in the Five Conversations Framework. Consider these benefits: You'd gain an instant snapshot of the organization through the climate review conversation. Once all the climate review conversations have taken place, the results can be analyzed. A report can be produced. I have an online web-based management support system that can do just this.[1]

The second conversation can identify all the strengths and talents across the organization. This information can be collated to build a capabilities statement for the business. The capabilities statement can be used for a range of purposes. It can be part of a succession plan. Or, the information can assist to redefine people's roles that better reflect the talents of the current workforce.

Data from the opportunities for growth and the learning and development conversations can be used to create a comprehensive training needs analysis across the organization.

And the innovation and continuous improvement conversation will undoubtedly unearth several easy-to-implement and cost-effective ideas to improve the efficiency and effectiveness of the business.

But I think the overriding benefit of the Five Conversations Framework is as a vehicle for fostering a better working relationship between management and workforce.

In the next chapter, we consider the content and other benefits of the framework I have introduced to you in this chapter.

The Top 10 Key Points …

1. The Five Conversations Framework focuses on individual and organizational performance.
2. The framework is designed to replace the traditional once-a-year performance review.
3. The Five Conversations Framework is based on five conversations between the leader and team member.
4. These five conversations are designed to last for approximately 20 minutes each.
5. These five conversations are designed to be less formal, more relaxed, more frequent, and more focused than the conventional once- or twice-a-year performance review.
6. The order of the conversations has a logic to it. The framework is based upon five key questions.
7. You gain a snapshot of the organization through the climate review conversation.
8. The second conversation identifies individual strengths and talents.
9. Data from the opportunities for growth and the learning and development conversations can be used to create a comprehensive training needs analysis across the organization.

10. The innovation and continuous improvement conversation will undoubtedly unearth several easy-to-implement and cost-effective ideas to improve the efficiency and effectiveness of the business.

Note

1. For more information about this online management system to support the Five Conversations Framework, please contact Tim at tim@winnersatwork.com.au

18

Rationale and Benefits of the Five Conversations Framework

> *While the five developmental conversations we discussed in Part II are standalone conversations, the Five Conversations Framework is a collection of performance discussions that work in tandem.*

In the previous chapter, the middle column of Table 17.1 shows the main theme for each of the five conversations. Each conversation for that month relates to the content in the third column. More detailed guidelines for each performance conversation—including the questions—are covered in the remaining chapters of Part III. In this chapter I want to concentrate on the rationale and benefits of this approach and framework.

While people I speak with are overwhelmingly in favor of this new framework and can see the value of having regular performance conversations, some academics and practitioners have been critical of my approach. A recent blogger says, for example, that he thinks the Five Conversations Framework is 'too soft.' He goes on to say that employees are expected to perform, and his concern is that by doing away with the formal appraisal, performance standards may drop. Any criticism of the framework is in relation to it being a substitute for the traditional performance review.

The idea that a conversation is a *soft* option compared with a formal appraisal is nonsense. Whether the approach is hard or soft will depend upon the way it's conducted, and the type of questions asked by the leader. While I agree that the Five Conversations Framework is less formal than the traditional appraisal in approach, I think that's a good thing. If the lack of formality encourages employees to more fully engage with their leader, then that's highly desirable. So, the issue shouldn't be whether it is soft or hard; the issue surely is whether it's effective in positively impacting performance in a sustainable way.

What's more, I think it's harder to have an ongoing dialog with an employee about specific aspects of their performance than to conduct the standard performance review once or twice a year. The frequency and focus of the five conversations ensures that issues needing attention are discussed regularly. And more importantly, these conversations are followed up. Although the new approach is less formal, it inspires two-way dialog that's more appealing.

In my experience, people who give this new approach a go are pleasantly surprised at how well it works.

> **Where the Rubber Meets the Road …**
>
> **Positive Feedback about the Five Conversations Framework**
>
> Most of the feedback from experiences of using the Five Conversations Framework has been very positive. For example, Alan Clark from the UK had this to say about the approach:
>
> *I want to start by saying that I very much like the approach of the five conversations. It represents a systematic approach and [is] a useful tool for obtaining the information the team leaders, top management, and HR professionals need to know. I for one am interested in using this approach. My personal experience with annual job appraisals is more positive than most, although I know there's a whole spectrum of good and bad practice out there. I think the contribution they make is partly a question of management style: a good manager with an open, participative style will adapt and use the process in a constructive manner. A good manager should also be collecting the information that is targeted by the Five Conversations Framework and if his or her current communication channels do not facilitate this exchange then they will benefit in my view by adopting the Five Conversations Framework.*[1]

I devote an entire chapter to each of these five conversations, as mentioned earlier. Below is the justification for each conversation.

Climate Review Conversation

A climate review assesses the current atmosphere in a workplace. It's mainly concerned with job satisfaction, morale, and communication. However, naturally, people's opinion about these matters fluctuates over the course of a year. It's important, though, to take a snapshot of your team occasionally.

These check-ins assist leaders to get a handle on the present state of the team. Information from these conversations can be a rich source of data for responsive remedial action.

Strengths and Talents Conversation

I'm sure you'd agree that most performance appraisals are fixated on what's going wrong. They focus, in other words, on weaknesses and usually neglect to discuss employee strengths. Tom Rath—in the #1 *Wall Street Journal* bestseller, *StrengthsFinder 2.0*—makes the claim that:

> Society's relentless focus on people's shortcomings has turned into a global obsession. What's more, we have discovered that people have several times more potential for growth when they invest energy in developing their strengths instead of correcting their deficiencies.[2]

Apart from being a far more positive place to start discussing performance—as Roth points out—building upon people's strengths has a higher payoff than working on overcoming their weaknesses. This doesn't mean that we shouldn't discuss deficiencies. We should. And that is why the third conversation is about opportunities for growth. But starting with a person's strengths makes perfect sense, don't you think?

This conversation is not just about identifying individual strengths—it's also about how they can be better utilized in their current or future roles. Are there tasks and projects they are presently not doing that would suit that person's aptitude? For instance, one of your team members has a talent for dealing with people but is presently stuck in an office looking at a computer screen all day. The conversation on strengths may acknowledge this strength. How the person's job can be restructured to accommodate more customer interface should be considered in this conversation. While learning about people's strengths is interesting and affirming, it offers little more, unless the strengths can be better applied in the workplace.

Opportunities for Growth Conversation

This conversation focuses on identifying specific areas for improved performance. It considers the question: *What areas does the team member need to improve?* In other words, this conversation provides an opportunity to consider where they may improve their own work performance. Once acknowledged, the leader and team member can discuss some tangible ways of improving productivity. This conversation is also about *how* they can improve their contribution. Agreed upon strategies can be adopted immediately, or at a time convenient.

Learning and Development Conversation

The learning and development conversation is designed to discuss the growth needs of the team member now and for the future. This may include formal opportunities, such as attendance at courses, programs, and seminars. Informal opportunities like skill development through coaching and mentoring should also be considered. This conversation establishes targets for personal and technical growth and career development. Having this conversation with all team members forms the basis of a coordinated training plan for the team. The leader can then prioritize and implement with more certainty learning and development opportunities that have currency and acceptance.

This conversation also offers a convenient opportunity for employees to discuss their career path. Since learning and development is future-focused, it opens the possibility for discussing how the leader can assist the individual to meet their broader career goals. There is some obvious crossover here with the coaching conversation (see Chap. 7) and encouraging conversation (see Chap. 13).

Like the strengths and talents and the opportunities for growth conversations, the learning and development conversation can guide and inform succession planning and keep high performers. Ambitious employees often leave an organization because they cannot envisage how they can fulfill their career goals. These star individuals may benefit from exploring career and development opportunities within the business with the active support of their manager. By aligning the leader's perceptions and expectations with career-minded team members, the leader obviously benefits too.

Innovation and Continuous Improvement Conversation

Conversations about innovation and continuous improvement opportunities are two dimensional. This conversation can contemplate practical means of improving the employee's efficiency. Also, it can explore team effectiveness.

In other words, this conversation considers ideas for developing new and better working arrangements for the individual and the organization. Discussing innovation and continuous improvement with all team members will undoubtedly lead to the immediate generation of several ideas. Some practical and cost-effective ways and means of tweaking or replacing current systems and processes within and beyond the team are inevitable.

Apart from systems and process development, some ideas are bound to progress the team's interactions with other teams and stakeholders. If considered feasible, they can be instigated.

Although each of these five conversations is a separate discussion, there are common threads and inevitable overlaps. In summary, the framework plays several important performance functions:

- It assesses current team climate;
- It audits strengths and talents and considers how they may be better deployed;
- It discusses opportunities for growth and supporting strategies;
- It identifies learning and development needs for a coordinated plan-of-action; and
- It explores potential innovative and continuous improvement ideas for adoption.

I'm sure you'd agree that these issues should be discussed. But they're often overlooked in the ambit of *busyness*. Even at performance review time, these performance matters are neglected, apart from possibly exploring growth opportunities. By breaking these important performance dimensions into a distinct set of themed conversations, the framework offers a concentrated emphasis and roadmap for individual and team performance improvement.

While the five developmental conversations we discussed in Part II are standalone conversations, the Five Conversations Framework is a collection of performance discussions that work in tandem. Although they too can be separate conversations, it's more effectively done as a framework. Ultimately, the Five Conversations Framework—with its comprehensiveness—can replace the traditional performance review.

To get the best from these five conversations, both leader and team member should prepare before meeting. Let me illustrate. Knowing the team (or organization) will be discussing innovation and continuous improvement in the month of June, team members are expected to offer suggestions to improve efficiency and effectiveness. They need to consider this before meeting. The leader should familiarize themselves with the questions to ask before meeting.

I have included the questions in the five subsequent chapters for each conversation. With both parties thoroughly prepared, the discussion undoubtedly will be more productive.

You may notice—like the five developmental conversations in Part II—that these performance conversations are people-centered. The leader's role is again to act as facilitator. *Facilitation* is one of those trendy words that's vague enough to cover almost anything. Quite simply, a facilitator's job within the context of a conversation is to make it easier for the individual to discuss the topic and their responses to it. By providing non-directive leadership, the facilitator helps the team member arrive at decisions that help them improve their performance.

The leader's role in these conversations is to assist and guide, not hinder and control. They ought to give the team member the opportunity to address the topic first. Fully consider and explore their contribution first before giving your input. The formal performance review on the other hand is manager-centered, despite all the rhetoric of it being a collaborative exercise. Let's be honest, it's the manager who sets the agenda, drives the appraisal, and whose opinion carries the most weight. The performance review is more about appraisal, whereas the Five Conversations Framework is more to do with developing the employee.

Regarding preparation, the team member can do this online. And managers too can document their actions from these conversations online. A management support system has been designed and developed to support the framework. Contact me for more information about this.[3] This system improves the quality and outcome of the conversation considerably.

As a quick summary, the Five Conversations Framework has several advantages over the traditional approach to appraising performance. I have summarized the main benefits below.

Ongoing Dialogue

The Five Conversations Framework facilitates a process of ongoing dialog. A leader can have five short conversations twice a year with each team member. That translates to two conversations on each topic annually. This ongoing dialog undoubtedly helps build a better working relationship. Healthy relationships as you now know are founded on trust. As we discussed in Part I, management gurus Kouzes and Posner state that, *Leadership is a relationship*.[3] Relationships are formed and maintained through regular, authentic dialog.

Open and Direct

The framework is a less formal system than the traditional performance review. It's more relaxed. Despite being more comfortable, the questions supporting the five conversations are direct, without being confrontational. Team members are encouraged in these conversations to be open and direct with their leader.

Flexible

These five conversations should be reasonably brief, lasting approximately 20 minutes each. They can happen within and around normal work duties. Whether they are held on- or off-site, it doesn't really matter. Leaders and team members can arrange to have these conversations when and where they find it mutually convenient. The only condition is that they occur regularly, preferably monthly. Compared with performance review, the framework is more flexible and easier to manage. This is likely to be more accommodating and less stressful.

Timely Information

Information originating from the conversations is timely. This is helpful for the leader and benefits the organization. Applied across the organization, the Five Conversations Framework provides a wealth of timely information for planning and development purposes. Being continual, the information is fresh and current. Feedback can therefore be acted upon in a timely and targeted way. Information from the traditional performance review is useful too. But it usually occurs once or twice a year.

To illustrate what I mean, consider the conversation for month five: innovation and continuous improvement. Assuming this conversation takes place across the organization in the month of January, there will be a plethora of ideas on making improvements in the workplace that are timely. Some ideas will certainly be good and some not-so-good. The good ones can be implemented immediately. Similar ideas may be raised at the annual or bi-annual review. But they'll likely get buried underneath all the other aspects of performance being discussed. They are inevitably forgotten and bypassed.

Relaxed

Five conversations of 20-minute duration—based on five specific topics every six months—is a more natural and relaxing approach than the big build-up and execution of the performance review discussion once or twice a year. The relaxed nature of these conversations doesn't necessarily mean they're not productive. Equally, because the traditional review is more formal doesn't necessarily mean it's more useful. Besides, there's lots of pressure to get through all the aspects of the formal appraisal discussion. Sometimes this leads to rushing or skirting over issues in the interests of completing the appraisal. Being thematically based, the framework—with adequate preparation from both parties—is more targeted. The pressure to cover all aspects in the formal appraisal is absent.

We have discussed the Five Conversations Framework in broad terms in this and the previous chapter. I've devoted a subsequent chapter to each of these five conversations in the framework. They can be discussed separately and not as part of the approach I've just described. We'll look at each conversation in more depth, starting with the climate review conversation.

The Top 10 Key Points …

1. A climate review assesses the current atmosphere in a workplace. It's mainly concerned with job satisfaction, morale, and communication.
2. The strengths and talents conversation is about identifying individual strengths and how they can be utilized now and in the future.
3. The opportunities for growth conversation focuses on strategies for improved performance. It provides team members with an opportunity to consider how they may improve their own work performance.
4. The learning and development conversation is designed to discuss the growth needs of the team member now and for the future.
5. The innovation and continuous improvement conversation is about practical ways and means of improving both the employee's efficiency and effectiveness and those of the organization.
6. The Five Conversations Framework facilitates a process of ongoing dialog.
7. The framework is a less formal system than the traditional performance review.
8. These conversations can be held within and around normal work duties.

9. Information originating from the conversations is timely.
10. Five conversations of 20-minute duration—based on five specific topics every six months—is a more natural and relaxing approach than the big build-up and execution of the performance review discussion once or twice a year.

Notes

1. Clarke, A. http://www.trainingjournal.com/blog/the-fiveconversations/.
2. Rath, T. (2007). Strengths finder 2.0. New York, Gallup.
3. I can be contacted at tim@winnersatwork.com.au about the Five Conversations Framework online management system.

19

Conversation 6: The Climate Review Conversation

The climate review conversation opens a door to enter a meaningful dialogue to discuss issues that are often not discussed and considered.

Maryanne sat down with her boss, Julie, to have their climate review conversation.

"Hi, Julie, I wanted to catch up with each of you in my team to see how things are going. Can I begin by asking you how you would currently rate your job satisfaction on a scale of 1 to 10, 10 being high and one being low?" Maryanne thought for a moment and then said, "I'd probably rate it a six now." "Okay, why do you rate it a six?"

"I mostly enjoy the work I do here, but ... " "Go on," Julie probed after a slight hesitation in Maryanne's response. "Well, I feel that the last project I was given was challenging and I felt that I was a bit out of my depths." "Okay, I knew it was demanding. I'm interested to know why you felt like that, Maryanne."

"Well, as you know, you asked me to report to the weekly team meeting with regular progress updates. I wasn't sure whether I covered all the information you required. I didn't get any feedback from you about what I should cover in these updates. That makes me feel I wasn't doing a thorough job. It had an impact on my job satisfaction at the time." "How could I have helped? What feedback would have been useful?"

"Well, I think if we had discussed the parameters of what I was—and wasn't—responsible for, it would have helped me a lot. For example, I wasn't sure whether you wanted me to report on the activities of the marketing team." "Okay, so if I'd sat down with you and not rushed and we'd discussed where the reporting boundaries were, that would have helped?" "Yes, absolutely. It would have made me feel more comfortable and know where I could and couldn't make decisions."

"Okay, in future, I will not rush things. Thinking back on this, it was clear in my head, but obviously not in yours. I will not make these assumptions in future. Thanks for that feedback. It's very useful for me to know this."

"I assume that when you rated your current job satisfaction a 6 out of 10, it would have been higher with a little more certainty around your roles and responsibilities?" Julie asked, for confirmation. "Yes, exactly. I enjoyed the project and I appreciated the opportunity of working on this, but I felt a little unsure of myself for the reasons I mentioned."

The conversation continued …

What's a Climate Review?

Of the 10 conversations in this book, the climate review may appear the most obscure. What's meant by *climate*? As you can guess, I'm not referring to the weather. Why does it need reviewing? A climate review is the perceptions employees have of their work and the working environment. It covers such aspects as job satisfaction, morale, and communication. These are the main components that make up the climate of any work-setting.

Employees can—and often do—have a wide range of perspectives and insights about the climate of their workplace. What's more, these attitudes can change in the twinkle of an eye for a host of reasons. Someone can feel great about their job this week and because of an irate customer, for instance, feel negative about it next week. The climate review conversation is a snapshot in time.

Conversations about a workplace's climate can be useful at any time, though. No organization will ever have the perfect climate; it can always be improved somehow. Climate review conversations can be useful when organizational productivity or output is low, for instance. This might be caused by high staff turnover, communication breakdowns, or organizational restructuring and general uncertainty about the future. In the good times, climate review conversations can insulate against complacency. So, in all circumstances this conversation has its place.

Even though managers get caught up in the day-to-day running of the business, conversations about satisfaction, morale, and communication are imperative in times of change too. The restructuring of a company, the introduction of a new product or service, relocating the company, major policy changes, rapid and sudden growth or declines, and significant changes in strategic direction are all suitable backdrops for a climate review conversation. In these circumstances, employees often feel alienated and don't have a voice. The climate review conversation in transformative environments and during big events gives employees a say in how they're feeling and what they're observing.

> **Where the Rubber Meets the Road …**
>
> **Employee Climate Surveys**
>
> Employee Climate Surveys are analyses of the observations and viewpoints of the employees of an organization that present a realistic depiction of the internal health of the company. The aim of every successful organisation is to effectively address its myriad problems and build an affirmative work environment. An Employee Climate Survey allows the organisation to function more competently by utilising inputs and satisfaction ratings from its workforce. The feedback solicited can be on a variety of issues such as quality of the working environment, interpersonal relations, staff development, customer service, and so on. The concerns and opinions expressed by employees help the organization understand and work with organizational members to inculcate positive changes and increase productivity.
>
> This process is essential especially during phases of diminished output or anytime the management believes that the organisational output has scope for improvement. Additionally, if there is a definite cause for dipping productivity, such as high staff renewal rate or ineffective communication, an Employee Climate Survey can help ascertain probable solutions to these problems and can be used to motivate employees and enhance job satisfaction.
>
> Employee Climate Surveys are valuable tools for facilitating development in times of organisational change, introduction of a new product or service, relocation, policy reforms or even a period of rapid development. In these circumstances, Climate Surveys give employees a mode of expression to help make these modifications as easy as possible.[1]

What value does this conversation add? A conversation reviewing climate serves several good purposes. We'll consider four key benefits.

Climate review conversations align values. They deliver very useful, timely information about the work environment. This type of conversation can be used to benchmark workplace climate. And tangible action can be taken from these conversations. Let's consider these benefits in more detail.

Value Alignment

What are the values communicated when having a conversation about climate? One obvious value communicated is that the leader is interested in the welfare of people at work. That message alone is valuable. A preparedness to discuss job satisfaction, morale, and communication indicates a leader wants better engagement with their team. Simply having a conversation doesn't mean more engagement, of course. But it does demonstrate a readiness to participate; it's an attempt to align perspectives, when done authentically. A climate review conversation signals a leader's intention to facilitate a more productive, harmonious work climate. The type of conversations a manager has (or doesn't have) sends a message of what they consider important (and unimportant).

Awareness resulting from these conversations can be quite insightful. For example, Fiona indicates that her job satisfaction is suffering because she isn't receiving timely information to compile her monthly report from someone in another team. Fiona discloses that she didn't feel confident to approach the other team leader about this consistent delay, although she knew she ought to. She also didn't feel comfortable raising it with Judy, her boss. Judy reassures Fiona that in future she should talk to her colleague in the other team to speed up the information process. Fiona was reassured by this understanding. Her job satisfaction got a shot in the arm from this simple affirmation.

Benchmarking Tool

Climate review conversations can be used to benchmark. By inviting a team member to rate their job satisfaction, morale and communication, you have some useful yardsticks. These benchmarks can be used in three ways. First, numbers give you a comparative analysis across your team. Who has the highest and lowest job satisfaction in the team? Although it ought to be said that the reasons behind the number are more important than the numbers themselves. A second use of these numbers is to conduct a comparative analysis with other teams in the organization. Are they significantly higher, lower, or on par with the rest of the organization? Why? Or, why not? And a third use is to compare these numbers with subsequent conversations with the same team member. Have they gone up or down? Why? The climate review conversation can be indicative of how individuals, teams, and managers are traveling generally. Organizations spend tens or hundreds of thousands of dollars every year on online surveys. Why don't we spare the cost and do this exercise face-to-face?

Here is an illustration of what I mean. If the aggregate rating out of 10 for morale is 5 and in six months' time the average is 7, it's reasonable to assume that morale has improved overall. As leader, this result may confirm your observations. But they give insight into *why* it has picked up. The ratings offer the leader a gateway to why perceptions have changed.

More Clarity

During these conversations you'll get a variety of responses. But there will be distinct themes. One overriding theme, for example, could be that people's understanding of what is expected of them is clearer. You can then build upon this realization. You may ask your team: *What—if anything—can I do to provide even more clarity around what I expect from you in your job?* Or, *What other factors can help us build morale in the team?* These questions can elicit constructive responses leading to simple, practical, implementable suggestions that further enhance the climate. After applying the change—such as visibly recognizing work of a high standard—you can test the impact of these tactics next time you have a series of climate review conversations.

By identifying areas of inefficiency—particularly in communication—and removing performance barriers, you're taking deliberate strides to humanizing the work-setting. Climate review conversations pinpoint areas of satisfaction and dissatisfaction; they assist the leader to nurture more harmony. This lifts performance.

Taking and Reviewing Action

And finally, leading on from the above point, climate review discussions can be used to take and review certain actions. While conversations can be engaging, unless something different happens as a result, they will sooner or later be regarded as a waste-of-time. When organizations roll-out the annual online engagement survey, the typical criticism is that nothing changes. Real changes because of these expensive survey exercises are often thin on the ground. After an initial review and discussion at the executive level, business as usual is characteristically the order of the day. At least with one-on-one communication, the leader's actions or lack of action is more apparent at the team level.

What Questions to Ask?

The following suggested questions cover job satisfaction, morale, and communication:

- *On a scale of 1 to 10 (10 being high and 1 low), how would you rate your current job satisfaction?*

The response to this question should be followed up with:

- *Why did you give it this rating?*

This question invites the team member to elaborate on their rating. For example, if someone rates their job satisfaction as a 9, their response maybe something like:

Because I believe we work well as a team and that gives me a lot of satisfaction personally.

Or, if they rate it a 1, their response maybe something like:

I don't feel I have the necessary resources or support to enjoy my job.

Whatever the reply, you have a number and explanation by asking these two simple questions. Job satisfaction ebbs and flows, as we know, depending on a host of factors. The rating and rationale nonetheless present a benchmark to compare with subsequent climate review conversations.

Here's the next suggested question:

- *On a scale of 1 to 10 (10 being high and 1 low), how would you rate morale in the department/section/team you are working in?*

Morale—also known as *esprit de corps*—is a term used to describe the capacity of people to maintain belief in the team or a goal, or even in oneself and others. In other words, morale refers to the level of individual faith in the collective benefit of the team toward the aims and objectives of the organization-at-large.

Why is this so important? Workplace events, such as heavy layoffs, cancellation of overtime, reduction in employee benefits, and poor union representation in a toxic workplace, affect morale. Other events influence workplace morale too, such as the abuse of sick leave entitlements by colleagues, low wages, and employee mistreatment. All these things have a negative impact on the bottom-line.

Like the job satisfaction question, the supplementary question is:

- *Why did you give it this rating?*

The response will raise some issues to consider. For example, if a team member rates morale a 9 out of 10, the team member may give a reason such as:

> People in our team work together to get the job done no matter what is in front of them.

On the other hand, someone rating morale as a 1 may say:

> Some people in our team are just not pulling their weight and that affects those that are.

Again, these ratings and responses serve as a useful benchmark for future climate review conversations.

For the topic of communication, two good questions are:

- *On a scale of 1 to 10 (10 being high and 1 low), how would you rate communication within our team?*
- *On a scale of 1 to 10 (10 being high and 1 low), how would you rate communication with other teams?*

The term *communication* can and does mean many things to many people. In their response, team members will interpret communication however they choose. Although the questions can be understood differently by each person, if does invite the employee the freedom to respond however they wish. It allows the team member to say what's top-of-mind regarding communication. And by doing so, it provides you with some insight of what your team view as important in the context of communication.

An employee may consider communication in terms of their working relationship with you, for instance. Or, communication could be interpreted as working with colleagues. These questions are purposely designed to be open-ended so as *not* to constrain the respondents' thinking. And this sheds light on the communication issues your team members consider important.

You'll notice that the two questions above have different emphases. The first one addresses communication *within* the team. And the second question is about communication with *other teams*. I think this is a reasonable distinction to make. After all, communication might be great within the team, but terrible with other teams, or vice versa.

Like the two previous sets of questions, the added question of *why* invites the other person to state the reason for their rating:

- *Why did you give it this rating?*

You'll likely get several different explanations. If someone rates it as 9 out of 10, they may say something like:

Our meetings are short, sharp, and to the point.

However, another person with a rating of 9 may have an entirely different reason for their score:

Senior management goes to great lengths to explain the reason for their decisions and how it will affect us in our team.

Instead, if someone rates it a 1, they may say:

We never get told anything and if we do, it's always at the last moment.

Or

I feel left out of the conversation at our staff meetings.

Both responses are completely different but nevertheless valid to the respondent.

These three sets of questions should be followed by one last question:

- *Is there anything else you would like to comment on regarding job satisfaction, morale, or communication?*

This invites your colleague with an opportunity to feel comfortable commenting on any other aspect of their job, morale, or communication.

In conclusion, the questions I'm proposing here encourage open dialogue between leaders and team members. It hopefully generates some solutions—

wherever needed—to improving organizational climate. Also, the climate review conversation offers valuable benchmarks to measure success. This conversation opens a door to enter a meaningful dialogue on matters that are rarely discussed.

In the next chapter, we'll consider the conversation on strengths and talents.

The Top 10 Key Points …

1. A climate review is the perceptions employees have of their work and the working environment.
2. It covers such aspects as job satisfaction, morale, and communication.
3. Climate review conversations can be useful when organizational productivity or output is low. This might be caused by high staff turnover, communication breakdowns, or organizational restructuring and general uncertainty about the future. In the good times, climate review conversations can insulate against complacency.
4. Climate review conversations align values.
5. This conversation can provide very useful, timely information about the work environment.
6. Climate review conversations can be used to benchmark.
7. Tangible action can be discussed and taken from these conversations.
8. Morale—also known as esprit de corps—is a term used to describe the capacity of people to maintain belief in the team or a goal, or even in oneself and others.
9. Communication can be viewed two ways: within and outside the team.
10. This conversation opens a door to enter into a meaningful dialogue on matters that are rarely discussed.

Note

1. http://www.authbridge.com/services/talent-solutions/retention-a-development-services/employee-climate-surveys.html.

20

Conversation 7: The Strengths and Talents Conversation

If you want to engage the hearts and minds of people at work, you need to give them the scope to apply their strengths and talents at work.

Mary entered Sandra's office with some trepidation, knowing that she was about to be appraised for her performance after her initial six months on the job. She is an accountant in a medium-sized professional services firm.

Sandra began the appraisal with an unusual question: "Now that you've been in this job for six months, what are the tasks you enjoy doing the most?" Mary was blindsided; she wasn't expecting this kind of question first up. She thought carefully for a moment and responded thoughtfully, "I guess most of the time I like dealing with our clients."

"Approximately how much of your day is taken up with client interaction?" Sandra asked. "Not too much; maybe one hour at the most." "What is it about the client contact that you enjoy, Mary?" "I enjoy interacting with them to provide a range of solutions to their problems. I find that it energizes me and I feel useful." "Yes, I agree. I think this is one of your strengths, Mary. I get great feedback regularly from some of our valued clients."

"How can we work together to provide you with the opportunity to do more of this client-interface? Could I delegate more of the routine accounting work to one of the administrative assistants in the office and move you into a client liaison role? Perhaps we could make you the first point of contact for client requests, and that may entail you being out on the road more. That won't happen overnight, but we can work toward this," suggested Sandra positively. "That would be great, Sandra. I would really appreciate that opportunity!"[1] The appraisal was pleasantly surprising for Mary.

The world of work—which mirrors society-at-large—is obsessed with spotting employees' weaknesses. We're socialized from an early age to focus on identifying and overcoming our weak points rather than appreciating and building upon our strengths. Despite this focus on weaknesses, people will always get a better return on their investment in time and effort from developing their innate talent compared with striving to overcome a flaw.

If I'm naturally good with numbers and less gifted with words, for instance, where should I concentrate my energies? I can improve and even get very good at writing with some serious practice, undoubtedly. But it'll require significantly more application than cultivating a natural talent. If I put the same application into mathematics, in other words, I'll dramatically accelerate my growth comparatively. Why? Because I've an innate aptitude for numbers. It's easy to learn than building a vocabulary—not to mention, more enjoyable and less stressful. So, it makes intuitive sense to develop our gifts, more so than we are led to believe.

Our Obsession with Strengthening Weaknesses

Think about it: All things being equal, spending an hour developing a strength or talent is a far better use of your time than spending an hour trying to correct a deficiency, assuming we are applying good learning strategies in both cases. You'll learn faster, gain greater traction, and be more efficient and effective building on a talent compared with trying to conquer a weakness. And you'll enjoy it more too! As the familiar saying goes: *What seems common sense isn't always common practice.*

We're told by our parents and teachers at school to lift our grades on subjects we struggle with and maintain the good grades we get in subjects that come more naturally to us. When we enter the workforce, the traditional performance appraisal devotes a disproportionate amount of time to our weak areas and very little—if any—time on what we do well. So, it's little wonder that by the time we are established in the workplace we're obsessed with 'fixing' our weaknesses and simultaneously take our talents for granted.

Let's revisit employee engagement from Part I. *Gallup* has surveyed over 10 million people worldwide since the 1990s on the topic of employee engagement; that is, how positive and productive people are at work.[2] Only a third of those surveyed 'strongly agreed' with the statement: *At work, I have the opportunity to do what I do best every day*. Of those who 'strongly disagreed' or 'disagreed' with the statement, that is, those who felt they didn't focus on what they do best, none were emotionally engaged in their job. The message is clear: If you want to engage the hearts and minds of people at work, you need to give them the scope to apply their strengths and talents at work.

To further illustrate my point, Gallup's research suggests that employees who are given the opportunity to utilize their strengths are considerably more committed to their work than those who aren't given the same chance. These same people who exercise their strengths at work report having a better quality of life than colleagues who don't get the same opportunity. I think it's clear that focusing on strengths has substantial advantages for everyone: the individual, the organization where they work, and society-at-large. This reinforces the argument for having regular conversations about strengths. Giving people a chance to use their innate talents at work can pay dividends for all.

I'm not suggesting that you turn a blind eye to people's weaknesses. The next performance conversation I cover in Chap. 21 does just that. My point is this: Leaders need to redress this imbalance of focusing on weaknesses by discussing strengths and talents equally.

Not only are traditional performance appraisals preoccupied with identifying weaknesses, managers are fixated with pouring resources and support into overhauling employee weaknesses. What's more, most learning and development programs are designed to address people's weak points. As Tom Rath in *Strengths Finder 2.0* puts it, these programs "help us to become who we are not."[3] If you're poor with numbers you're sent on a course to develop accounting skills, for example. Or, if you're appraised as being weak at dealing with people, you're sent on a course to boost your *emotional intelligence*. Our whole life is programmed to building up our weak spots. This takes the focus away from capitalizing on our natural aptitudes.

We're socialized to believe it's virtuous to be working on our shortcomings. As I said in *The End of the Performance Review*:

> Our heroes in society are those who have overcome massive obstacles. People who excel despite a physical disability, individuals who triumph over barriers such as age, discrimination, and economic circumstances. Our lives are filled with such stories. These stories are undeniably inspirational. But they teach us that overcoming obstacles is more virtuous than capitalizing on our strengths and talents.[4]

On the other hand, we take for granted those with natural talent. We don't value the blood, sweat, and tiers put into harnessing our gifts. We don't see—or want to see—what we call in Australia—the *hard yakka* put into the practice of perfecting talent.

> **Where the Rubber Meets the Road ...**
>
> **I must at least try**
>
> In June 1985, two British mountaineers, Joe Simpson and Simon Yates, made the first-ever ascent of the west Face of the 21,000-foot, snow-covered Siula Grande mountain in Peru. It was an exceptionally tough assault; but nothing compared with what was to come. Early in the descent, Simpson fell and smashed his right knee. Yates could have abandoned him but managed to find a way of lowering him down the mountain in a series of difficult drops blinded by snow and cold. Then Simpson fell into a crevasse and Yates eventually had no choice but to cut the rope, convinced that his friend was now dead.
>
> In his subsequent book on the climb, entitled *Touching the Void*, Joe Simpson wrote:
>
> "As I gazed at the distant moraines, I knew that I must at least try. I would probably die out there amid these boulders. The thought didn't alarm me. It seemed reasonable, matter-of-fact. That was how it was. I could aim for something. If I died, well, that wasn't so surprising., but I wouldn't have just waited for it to happen. The horror of dying no longer affected me as it had in the crevasse. I now had the chance to confront it and struggle against it. It wasn't a bleak, dark terror any more, just fact, like my broken leg and frostbitten fingers and I couldn't be afraid of things like that. My leg would hurt when I fell and when I couldn't get up I would die."
>
> The survival of Yates was extraordinary. That Simpson somehow found a way of climbing out of the crevasse after 12 hours and then dragged himself six miles back to camp, going three days and nights without food or drink, losing three stone, and contracting ketoacidosis in the process, would be the stuff or heroic fiction if it were not true. Indeed, six operators and two years later, he was even back climbing. All because, against all odds, he tried ...[5]

Inspirational stories, such as the one above, perpetuate a powerful myth in our society. Conquering shortcomings is romanticized to such an extent that it's considered an essential element of our culture. Movies, books, TV series, and the like are filled with stories and revelations of the 'underdog' beating the odds. This leads us to idolize those people who've succeed, despite their lack of natural ability. There's no room for celebrating individuals who've exercised their innate talents for achievement; except to say they're somehow lucky. We therefore try to emulate the underdog. We believe that the way ahead is to master our shortcomings. Exploiting our strengths is a secondary consideration—if considered at all. Unfortunately, though, minimizing our weaknesses instead of building upon our strengths is the path of *most* resistance.

So, it's little wonder that this idea is customary when assessing work performance. This conventional approach raises these kinds of questions:

- What are my team members' weaknesses?
- How can they overcome these?
- What can the organization do to help?

We don't really consider the alternative questions:

- What are my team members' strengths?
- How can they use these strengths in their work?
- What can the organization do to help?

The traditional performance appraisal system is more concerned with the first—and not the second—set of questions.

The Rule of the Three Ps

A final word on strengths: What people enjoy doing is a reasonable indicator of where their strengths lie. There's a saying about the three Ps that goes like this: We *practice* what we *prefer* and ultimately become *proficient* at it. Our preferences are a good clue to what our strengths and talents are. What do you *prefer* to do in your current role? Which tasks do you enjoy the most? Given a choice, what would you rather do in your current role? These questions are a useful starting point to understanding our natural inclinations.

What Questions to Ask?

Based on the three Ps concept, a useful question to start the conversation on strengths and talents is:

- *What tasks do you enjoy doing most in your current job?*

Although people ought to be given an opportunity to consider this question before the conversation takes place, you may need to prompt them or offer your observations of what you consider to be the team member's favored activities.

The follow-up question is:

- *Why do you enjoy those sorts of task?*

This question provides more clarification of the team member's strengths. For example, in answer to the first question, they may say:

I enjoy liaising with customers.

When asked why, they may simply say something like:

I enjoy interacting with people.

This may suggest a natural inclination for selling and promotion. You can discuss this response further by asking:

- *In your current role, how can we work together to provide you with more opportunity to use your strength(s)?*

There may not be a straightforward answer to this question. The employee may, for example, be an accounts clerk and most of their work is dealing with figures. But on reflection—and after discussing this with the accounts clerk—the manager might recognize that their employee's talents are best suited to working with clients rather than doing the accounts. While you may not be able to do anything about this situation in the short term, you can start planning to reshape the team member's role to maximize their talents for the future.

Strategies for Reshaping Roles

Leaders ought to consider some tried and proven strategies for exercising the talents of the people they lead. These strategies may include:

- job rotation;
- job enrichment;
- job enlargement; and
- multi-skilling.

Let us briefly consider these four options to guide and inform the strengths and talents conversation.

Job Rotation

Job rotation is designed to give an employee a breadth of exposure to the entire operation by giving them a chance to do one or several different roles for a designated period. Job rotation is also practiced for acquiring more knowledge and insight into the processes of an enterprise. For the right person it stimulates engagement and job satisfaction through exposure to a variety of skills and activities. The term *job rotation* can also mean the scheduled exchange of people in regional or international offices.

The employees I speak with who are involved and suited to job rotation assignments generally say they are challenged, feel more fulfilled, and develop a greater sense of obligation to and understanding of their current organization. And managers I've spoken with who have adopted job rotation as a strategy say it has increased employee effectiveness and helps with their retention too. This is one way of better utilizing talent.

Job Enrichment

Job enrichment is a second way of motivating an employee by giving them increased responsibility and variety in their job. Many employers believe that money is the only true motivating factor—if you want to get more performance from an employee. While it's probably true for a small percentage of people, most employees—as we covered in Part I—enjoy stimulating work and want to be appreciated for the work they do. Job enrichment—allowing employees to have more control in planning their work and deciding how the work should be accomplished—is another way of increasing their autonomy. By tapping into the natural desire most employees have for doing a good job, to be appreciated for their contributions, and feel a sense of belonging—job enrichment is a good strategy.

There are many different types of job enrichment activities and programs that you can use to encourage a team member's participation and foster the right environment for their human spirit to thrive. In any case, the purpose of job enrichment is to improve the quality of an employee's work experience and to flexibly deploy their strengths in several contexts.

Job Enlargement

Job enlargement refers to increasing the scope of a job by extending the range of its duties and responsibilities. This approach is the antithesis of specialization and the division of labor. Specialist employment practices organize work into small, clearly defined units, each performed repetitively by the job-holder. The boredom and alienation caused by the division of labor can lead to disengagement, as we discussed in Chap. 1. Job enlargement seeks to reverse the process of specialization and create an environment where an employee finds their work more purposeful.

There's a difference between job enrichment and job enlargement. Job enrichment means improvement—or an increase in personal growth with the help of upgrading and development. Whereas, job enlargement means adding more responsibilities and increasing workload. Through job enrichment, satisfaction can be derived from developing personally. The satisfaction from job enlargement comes from the challenges of added responsibilities, such as taking on supervisory duties. Both strategies can build upon the natural aptitudes of team members.

Multi-skilling

Multi-skilling—a fourth approach—is a coordinated method to train or coach team members to undertake a greater variety of work tasks beyond their current job description. Although I should point out that a multi-skilled employee isn't the same as a generalist. A multi-skilled employee is expected to be competent in more than one function and might be described as a versatile specialist. The challenge here is to balance flexible deployment with a set of core competencies.

A successful multi-skilling program must deal with five key questions:

- What skills are open to a multi-skilling program?
- What type of training is required?
- How will the work be managed?
- How will the work be executed?
- When and how will the work be evaluated?

This is another approach to expose the talents of team members.

Job rotation, job enrichment, job enlargement, and multi-skilling can boost engagement and exercise strengths and talents.

In summary, the strengths and talents conversation is based on the premise that developing and utilizing innate talent can be a more effective approach than trying to vanquish vulnerabilities. As I point out, society has conditioned us to concentrate on the later.

We will now move our attention to discuss the opportunities for growth conversation.

The Top 10 Key Points …

1. The world of work—which mirrors society-at-large—is obsessed with spotting employees' weaknesses.
2. All things being equal, spending an hour developing a strength or talent is a far better use of your time than spending an hour trying to correct a deficiency, assuming we are applying good learning strategies in both cases.
3. Giving people a chance to use their innate talents at work can pay dividends for all.
4. Leaders need to redress this imbalance of focusing on weaknesses by discussing strengths and talents equally.
5. Most learning and development programs are designed to address people's weak points.
6. The traditional performance appraisal system is more concerned with addressing questions around employee weaknesses.
7. What people enjoy doing is a reasonable indicator of where their strengths lie.
8. The rule of the three Ps states that we practice what we prefer and ultimately become proficient at it.
9. A useful question to start the conversation on strengths and talents would be: What tasks do you enjoy doing most in your current job?
10. The strategies of job rotation, job enrichment, job enlargement, and multi-skilling can boost engagement and maximize an employee's strengths and talents.

Notes

1. Baker, T. (2013). *The end of the performance review: A new approach to appraising employee performance.* London: Palgrave Macmillan.
2. Rath, T. (2007). *Strengths finder 2.0.* New York: Gallup.
3. Ibid.
4. Baker, T. (2013). *The end of the performance review: A new approach to appraising employee performance.* London: Palgrave Macmillan.
5. Simpson, J. (1988). *Touching the void: The true story of one man.* New York: HarperCollins.

21

Conversation 8: The Opportunities for Growth Conversation

Good leaders give regular, ongoing feedback.

Craig was about to have a potentially challenging and stressful conversation with Mary, one of his supervisors. He'd arranged to meet Mary in a private, comfortable room away from his office.

Craig had frequently been told about the unnecessarily abrupt way Mary spoke to her team members when she wanted something done. Besides, Craig had witnessed this first-hand on several occasions. He felt that this was one area Mary needed to address immediately.

Mary was inclined to tell people what to do—rather than ask them—and her work colleagues understandably resented this. Craig was concerned that Mary mightn't accept this criticism in a constructive way. He was apprehensive about this conversation. He tried a different tack.

Mary arrived punctually, and Craig got straight to the point, "Mary, if there is one area you believe is an opportunity for growth, what is it?" After a lengthy and awkward pause, she replied, "I can't seem to get my team members to show any initiative. I have to do all the thinking for them."

Craig responded with a question, "Okay. Can you elaborate on this so that I fully understand what you mean?" "Well, I find myself telling people what to do when I'd rather they show some initiative and do what they're paid to do," replied an exasperated Mary. "What do you think the reason for this is, Mary?" "I don't know really," came Mary's answer, with a sigh.

"What are the consequences of this?" "Well, I find I have to raise my voice and direct people to do what they should know already," was Mary's agitated response. "When you raise your voice, what happens?" "People walk off in a huff usually and don't listen to me." "I see. I guess you're not happy about that reaction, then?" "No, I'm not at all."

"What would you like to happen?" "I'd like them to listen to me and just do what needs to be done without any argument." "Well, what can you do differently to get this result?" "I don't really know."

"Have you tried asking them without raising your voice?" "Yeah, but that doesn't work." "When was the last time you did this?" "I can't remember. I get so frustrated I can't help raising my voice." "But you say that's not working?" Craig replied patiently. "No, it definitely doesn't work, but it's the only way."

"Can I suggest you try asking them in a calm manner and see what happens? It's worth a go, isn't it?" "Well, nothing else is working, Craig!" Mary responded, with resignation in her voice.

"So, I have your commitment to give it another go?" "Yeah, I suppose so," sighed Mary.

"Is there anything I can do to help?" "No, not really. You've been helpful just listening to me. I'll just have to control myself and do as you suggest." "Good. Come back and tell me how you get on, won't you?"

Apart from the strengths and talents conversation we discussed in the previous chapter, the other conversation directly related to performance is the opportunities for growth conversation. The other three conversations in the framework are indirectly about performance.

Since the opportunities for growth conversation centers on areas for improvement, it can sometimes be the most challenging conversation in the framework. I'm therefore going to share some ideas to support you. Many of these guidelines relate to the other four conversations too.

This conversation is one element—although an important element—of managing performance. But it's the one aspect of performance management that seems to get all the attention and books written about it.

In a perfect world, all performance conversations would positively impact the performance, motivation, and commitment of employees. They would also align everyone's effort with the strategic direction of the organization. The standard performance review, however, has the opposite effect sometimes. They can hurt, demoralize, and anger the recipient. The result can be—from that point forward—that the person being appraised does no more than the bare minimum without getting sacked. I'm sure you've seen this happen.

The opportunities for growth conversation should happen regularly—not once a year. I'd suggest having this conversation at least twice a year.

Information to guide and inform this conversation should come from a variety of sources. You can start perhaps with the team member's observations about their own performance. Personal reflection is an often-untapped avenue of information. Other information should come from secondary sources, such as people with whom the team member interacts with. Yet another source is your observations. Using all three sources—theirs, others, and yours—can be useful.

Here are some tips on preparing for your conversation. Effective conversations—whether it's this one, or any of the other—are built on sound preparation, putting aside corridor conversations. Three critical points you need to think about are:

- an awareness of their work performance;
- the timing and place of the conversation; and
- your frame-of-mind.

Let us look briefly at each of these.

Awareness

It's helpful to have a sound knowledge of the team member's work performance. This awareness includes, wherever possible, observing their behavior and the outcomes of that behavior. If you can't see it first-hand, rely on other sources. Whichever way you turn, you're looking for critical incidents that illustrate areas of improvement.

If you're concerned about a lack of adherence to meeting deadlines, then find an incident or two where they were late in completing a report or getting back to a customer, for example. What were the consequences of their tardiness? These incidents and their negative impact exemplify your concern—and hopefully theirs—about meeting deadlines for the future.

Timing

Setting a time and finding a place for the conversation can have an often-underestimated bearing on the success of the conversation. The time and place ought to be convenient for both parties. It should allow sufficient time—without interruption—to have a thorough discussion. It's not a good idea, for instance, to conduct this conversation across your desk, while the phone is constantly ringing and people are coming in and out of your office like a busy elevator on a Friday afternoon. I strongly encourage you not to have any of the 10 conversations sitting behind your desk. Use comfortable chairs set at a 90-degree angle to each other or sitting at adjacent sides of a table. This is more conducive to good conversation. Ensuring eye level is roughly equal (same-height chairs) also helps. These factors set the tone for a productive and relaxed conversation.

Frame-of-mind

The right frame-of-mind is respectful and inquiring, not disrespectful and closed-minded. You should be courteous, based hopefully on a professional working relationship with a history of consistent, considerate, fair treatment, balanced feedback, and communication. Demonstrating a genuine concern for the other person's wellbeing and development is a good start. This involves you keeping an open-mind—which is more difficult than it may seem.

Let's now look at some other key considerations during this and other conversations. The most critical things you need to be aware of are to:

- consider the ideal outcome of the conversation;
- allow the team member to reflect on their own development first;
- offer your feedback;
- be objective;
- use a problem-solving approach;
- think about all factors affecting performance; and
- ask questions and listen.

There are other considerations. But these are significant for all productive performance conversation.

The Ideal Outcome of the Conversation

As the late Dr. Stephen Covey states in his brilliant book, *The 7 Habits of Highly Successful People*, "Begin with the end in mind."[1] What this means in practice is to steer every comment and observation your team member makes toward the desirable outcome.

For example, a team member might say, "I'm now using a 'to-do list,'" in response to admitting their need to be better organized with a clearer focus on priorities. Your response should be along the lines of, "How is a to-do list going to help you stick to your priorities?" rather than simply saying "Good." It's always helpful to tie their response back to the goal—in this case to be better organized.

Allow Them to Reflect on Their Performance

Inviting people to consider their growth opportunities is generally a good place to begin this conversation. Ask the team member what areas they believe improvement is needed before offering your observations. If their opinion is the same as yours, then that is a good start. You can then agree and guide the conversation to what they could do to improve and how you can assist them to do that.

Alternatively, if your perspective is different, listen to their view with authenticity (easier said than done, I know!) first. Then suggest to them that you discuss your differing perception. Irrespective of what they say, show respect and listen without interrupting them. This builds trust; one of the five pillars of the authentic conversations we discussed in Chap. 5.

The key message is to seek-out the common ground, if feasible. A good rule of thumb is to agree wherever possible and reframe anything the team member says that is overly self-critical. People are often their own worst critics.

Offer Feedback

Good leaders give regular, ongoing feedback. The growth conversation is an opportunity to summarize or reinforce your expectations. All feedback is best delivered in the form of *Situation*, *Behavior*, and *Impact*. Briefly describe the situation; that is, when and where the unsuitable behavior is taking place. Then proceed to outline the unhelpful behavior. Follow-up with the negative impact this behavior causes.

For example:

> Our regular Monday morning staff meetings are for sharing ideas and problem-solving *[situation]*. In the last three meetings, I've noticed that you have criticized four suggestions that Matthew and Karen have raised without offering a possible alternative solution *[behavior]*. By doing this, you are affecting morale, and others may not want to contribute their ideas *[impact]*.

Using this framework draws attention to their behavior and lessens the chance the other person will interpret the negative feedback as a personal attack. It's quite possible the recipient may have a different perception of the impact of their behavior. This conflicting observation could be because they've been paying attention to other priorities. In response to the feedback above, for instance, the employee may respond by stating that they were trying to be constructive—they were pointing out that the ideas raised haven't worked in the past. You can then discuss the opposing perspectives you and they have. This "Situation, Behavior, and Impact" framework is a more considered and objective approach than just labeling the behavior as negative.

Be Objective

Being objective means separating the person from the performance issue. The person isn't the problem—the behavior is the problem. It's important for you to separate the person's intentions from the outcomes of the situation. This can be done by acknowledging that you believe their intentions were constructive (or at least not destructive). Assuming the team member had good intentions—despite their unhelpful behavior—helps you to consider other approaches without them becoming defensive.

Use a Problem-solving Approach

Instead of apportioning blame or being fixated on the performance issue, a more constructive tactic is to explore other ways of behaving. Your job is to highlight the gap between where they are and where you want them to be.

Invite the team member to consider the reasons for the difference between their intentions and the outcome. This may mean acknowledging barriers beyond their control. Further, make a commitment to do what you can to remove those barriers in future—if that's possible. In return for this promise, you should encourage the team member to identify how they could do things differently next time. It's not helpful to dwell on the past, other than to explore the necessary learning from it. One of the five pillars of authentic conversation is building for the future (see Chap. 6). This is the essence of using a problem-solving approach.

Think About All Factors

The *ABC analysis* is a good way to explore all the factors associated with poor performance. All behaviors (B) have antecedents (A); that is, triggers and consequences (C). When working out how to adjust unhelpful behaviors, analyze what the factors may be and pay attention to subtle external antecedents. Don't assume that the trigger for a behavior is wholly about the person. Try also to analyze the consequences that might be reinforcing the unhelpful behavior.

For example, if you have observed that your colleague's last three reports contained numerous mistakes (B), ask them why this has happened. They may say they were rushed and—after further probing from you—point out that the delay was a result of someone not getting necessary information to them to finish the report (A). Due to the information being late, they had less time to thoroughly proof-read the reports (C). Notwithstanding that this could simply be an excuse, the discussion then moves to how to safeguard receiving timely information in future.

Based on an expectation that the team member will receive timely information in future, ask them to commit to thoroughly proof-reading the final draft. You've done two constructive things here. First, you've gained their commitment to proof-read their reports (assuming you get that commitment). And second, you've exposed a potentially plausible explanation for the substandard report writing.

Ask Questions and Listen

My advice is to listen more and talk less in this, or any other developmental or performance conversation. And the way to do this is by asking questions, particularly open-ended questions. Actively listening to the other person's responses means paraphrasing or summarizing what you've heard. By asking open-ended questions and actively listening, you demonstrate an interest in and understanding of their opinions and priorities. This is a sound basis for helping them set or reset performance goals.

As the saying goes: *People don't care how much you know until they know you care*. And the best and most effective way to demonstrate that you *care* is to encourage the other person to talk. Giving them an opportunity to elaborate by asking questions and then summarizing what you've said. Again, this builds trust.

These are the fundamental considerations needed to facilitate a successful performance conversation.

> **Where the Rubber Meets the Road ...**
>
> **Why Asking Questions So Important?**
>
> Andrew Sobel and Jarold Panas in their book *Power Questions: Build Relationships, Win New Business, and Influence Others*,[2] reinforce the importance of questions:
> Asking thoughtful questions enables you to learn about the other person, be they a client, your boss, a colleague, or a friend. Sometimes we can spend a lot of time with someone without really knowing anything about them. Questions enable you to connect. And for what it's worth, they make you look smart. When a relationship is all business and there is no real personal connection, it lacks heart and soul. And therefore, you are a commodity—a kind of fungible expert-for-hire. A client—or your boss—can trade you out for a new model with no remorse or emotion. But when you've connected personally, the situation is transformed because clients stick with people they like. Bosses hold on to team members they feel passionately about. Personal relationships build loyalty in a way that expertise or brilliance doesn't!

What Questions to Ask?

A good starting question in the opportunities for growth conversation is:

- *If there is one area where you believe you have an opportunity for growth, what would it be?*

This question offers your team member to critically reflect on their own performance. The question is stated in such a way as to invite the possibility that they don't see any room for improvement in their current role. Of course, there's always room for improvement. But the question stops you immediately zeroing in on an area you're concerned about.

It's not necessarily helpful to start with: "Now, I have a real concern about your inability to manage your time and priorities. What are you going to do about this?" This kind of statement and question invites defensiveness and even, hostility. Them being over-protective is unhelpful, regardless of how *right* you may be about your claim!

On the assumption that the team member has mentioned something worthy of further discussion, the follow-up question might be:

- *Can you elaborate on this so that I understand what you mean?*

Conversation 8: The Opportunities for Growth Conversation

This offers them an opportunity to explain in their own words what they mean. It's entirely possible that you know what they mean—without hearing their explanation—but this isn't the point. The point is to fully and respectfully understand the employee's perspective on the performance matter and to get them to *own* their behavior.

Here, it's tempting for you to jump in and say: "I agree!" if you do agree or no "I don't agree" if you don't. By making this sort of judgment, you've effectively closed off the possibility of discussing their perspective any further.

Remember ABC. Invite them to explain the behaviors (B) that they consider need improving. Let's imagine that your colleague says the following:

I think I need to improve my computer skills

to your initial question: *If there is one area where you believe you have an opportunity for growth, what would it be?* On your request to elaborate, they then say,

I've had trouble with *Excel* and I use it regularly in my work.

When you understand their perspective fully, ask, "Why do you have trouble with Excel?" (A). The team member may reply by saying they haven't been given the opportunity to learn this software properly. And finally, you ask, "How's this affecting your work?" (C). They may claim that it takes twice as long to produce spreadsheets.

The next question, once you've fully understood their perspective on the question, *can you elaborate on this so that I understand what you mean?* is:

- *What can we do to improve this performance?*

Notice that I use the term *we* in this question. The implication of using the term *we* is that you are prepared, wherever possible, to help the team member and support their growth. Ultimately, you want the people you lead to take full responsibility for their own growth. But employees also have an expectation that their manager will support them to do so—or at least not put roadblocks in their path.

I'd suggest tackling no more than two performance issues in the one conversation. So, the next question could be:

- *Apart from that, what other area in your current role do you think provides an opportunity for growth?*

You then repeat the sequence of questions.

It's better to tackle two areas for growth thoroughly than several in a superficial manner. Of course, you can respectfully *agree to disagree* with your team member's opinion at any time in the conversation. But the important point here is that—through a series of questions—you are assisting the team member to take ownership for their performance.

If you feel there are other areas of performance where the employee can improve, a statement like:

- *Can I suggest another area you might consider is …?*

From here, you can offer a couple of critical incidents that illustrate your point.

Then ask them for their response with these questions:

- *What's your opinion about this?*
- *What behaviors do you believe are contributing to this?*

If they're on the same page as you, then it's a matter of guiding them to find a way to lift their performance in that area.

On the other hand, if they don't agree with you, then the contrasting perspectives need to be discussed. In these circumstances, you need to be firm, but respectful. It's important you explain your reasons for disagreeing. This can be done by explaining or reiterating your standards and indicating where you think they are falling short. Don't hesitate to ask them if they're clear about your expectations and how you can work together to improve their performance.

In conclusion, the opportunities for growth conversation directly relates to performance. It can be the most challenging of the 10 conversations in this book. The goal is to guide the employee to better performance.

In the next chapter, we look at the learning and development conversation.

The Top 10 Key Points …

1. Apart from the strengths and talents conversation we discussed in the previous chapter, the other conversation directly related to performance is the opportunities for growth conversation.

Conversation 8: The Opportunities for Growth Conversation

2. Since the opportunities for growth conversation centers on areas for improvement, it can sometimes be the most challenging conversation in the framework.
3. In terms of preparation, the critical points you need to think about are an awareness of their work performance, the timing and place of the conversation, and your frame-of-mind.
4. Setting the time and place for the conversation can have an often-underestimated bearing on the success of the conversation.
5. The right frame-of-mind is respectful and inquiring, not disrespectful and closed-minded.
6. The most critical things to be aware of during the conversation is to consider the ideal outcome of the conversation, allow the team member to reflect on their own development first, offer your feedback, be objective, use a problem-solving approach, think about all factors affecting performance, and ask questions and listen.
7. The growth conversation is an opportunity to summarize or reinforce your expectations.
8. A good starting question in the opportunities for growth conversation is, *If there is one area where you believe you have an opportunity for growth, what would it be?*
9. On the assumption that the team member has mentioned something worthy of further discussion, the follow-up question might be: *Can you elaborate on this so that I understand what you mean?*
10. The next question, once you've fully understood their perspective on the question, can you elaborate on this so that I understand what you mean? is, *What can we do to improve this performance?*

Notes

1. Covey, S.R. (2004). The 7 habits of highly successful people. London: Simon & Schuster.
2. Sobel, A. & Panas, J. (2012). Power questions: Build relationships, win new business, and influence others. New Jersey: Wiley.

22

Conversation 9: The Learning and Development Conversation

> *We learn from watching others, from experience, or from reflecting on that experience; we can learn through trial and error and learning can take place through discussion.*

Julie is the newly-appointed executive manager of learning and development for a large bank. She is charged with the responsibility of revamping the bank's approach to inducting customer service representatives (CSRs) in retail banking services. After looking at the high turnover rates and gathering information from the learning and development conversation across the company, she decided it was time to act.

From what she heard, the bank has had a challenge reducing high rates of turnover in CSRs in their first 12 weeks of employment. Employees told their managers in these conversations that they lacked confidence in their skills-set and knowledge of the bank's products and services. Changing the induction program was the place to start, Julie concluded.

From a learning perspective, the new induction program enabled participants to better analyze situations and source information quickly. This approach, supported by continuous coaching, involved a partnership between the participant, their branch manager, and an experienced CSR 'buddy.' With this backing, newly appointed CSRs were expected to take ownership of their learning and understanding of the bank's products and services. Additionally, new inductees would work with their branch manager to identify their strengths and areas of improvement through daily check-ins, debriefs, and feedback sessions.

Collaborative learning, using problem-based learning, simulations, and research was the core of the induction program. During the off-the-job learning periods, the new recruits worked in learning groups and explored customer scenarios they would likely encounter in real life. They were encouraged to analyze situations, explore how they might respond, and complete customer transactions using simulations or role plays.

After 12 months, the CSR induction program delivered an 8 per cent reduction in voluntary turnover.[1]

Following the strengths and talents and opportunities for growth conversations, you're ready to discuss team members' learning and development opportunities. From the previous two conversations, several ideas and strategies for capitalizing on the strengths and overcoming shortcomings have hopefully arisen. These ideas need consolidating into a learning and development plan. This chapter looks at the learning and development conversation and how to progress some of these thoughts from the previous conversations.

As we've discussed, learning is essential for individual and organizational success in a precipitously transforming world. Well-timed, targeted, effective learning experiences can unquestionably make a big difference to the bottom-line. Employees too now expect their employer to make a reasonable attempt to support their learning and development needs.

Not all learning is done in a classroom. Most learning takes place casually on the job. Yet, many people still think of learning as training, done formally in a classroom. And so, the conversation on learning and development should go beyond the question: *What training courses would you like to do this year?*

What is Learning and Development?

There's a fundamental difference between training and learning—training is part of learning, but learning is not just about training. Training implies an expert imparting their knowledge and skills to a group of participants. Learning, on the other hand, can take place anywhere, at any time, with anybody. We learn from watching others, from experience, or from reflecting on that experience; we can learn through trial and error and learning can take place through discussion. These are all ways we make sense of the world and develop as human beings.

Training is typically a structured event—or a series of events—led by a trainer and about a specific topic. While training is trainer-centered, learning is learner-centered. With learning, the attention is on the experience of learning rather than the action of the trainer. Learning can take place in a wide variety of ways, whereas training usually takes place in a classroom. Learning and development is a more comprehensive descriptor than training, since its scope is broader and its focus is on the person doing the learning.

Performance management mostly relies on training as one of its main solutions to optimize performance. *What training courses would you like to undertake over the next 12 months?* is a common question we ask during a performance appraisal. A better question perhaps is: *What would you like to learn over the next 12 months?* Or better still: *How do you want to develop over the next 12 months?* The latter two questions are learner-centered and encourage the recipient to consider themselves and their own development rather than what's out there in the world of training.

Once we've established what the team member wants to learn and how they wish to develop, the question to consider then is: *What is the best way to develop these skills and attributes?* The leader acts as the facilitator and problem-solver for the team member's learning, rather than a manager producing a shopping list of training courses and programs.

The obstacle of formal training is that it's too orientated around building technical skills and competencies. There are three dimensions of learning and development:

- technical-centered;
- person-centered; and
- problem-centered.

All three approaches have their place in a comprehensive learning and development program.

Let us briefly define each dimension.

Technical-centered

The technical-centered dimension is concerned with acquiring skills and competencies that have a direct application to a job-holder's current or future job. This is by far the most recognized form of learning. Organizations devote most of their learning budget and resources building technical skills and capabilities. Since there's a direct link between training and the job, the technical-centered approach is easier to measure in terms of its effectiveness. The success of technical-centered learning is typically assessed by observing the participant on the job doing the technical task they've been trained to do.

This form of learning can usually be applied immediately on the job, which is another attraction of the technical-centered approach.

For instance, a project manager—who learns project management skills—can apply the learning in their day-to-day job immediately. The manager can easily observe whether these skills and capabilities have been applied to improve the employee's capacity to manage projects. This ability to observe changes on the job is one of the main reasons a technical-centered approach is the most widely recognized and popular dimension of learning.

But it only covers one dimension of learning.

Person-centered

Person-centered learning—more commonly referred to as personal development—is concerned with improving the person. This approach has an indirect impact on workplace performance. It has gained more prominence over the past 30 years or so and is now recognized as a legitimate dimension of workplace learning and development. It's based on the belief that by improving the person, you improve their ability to perform the job. However, its impact is more difficult to assess in overall work performance. Courses such as time management, goal-setting, and stress management are examples of the person-centered dimension. Despite its less direct impact on work performance, compared with the technical-centered approach and the challenge in measuring its success, personal development can have a positive impact on a job-holder's ability to do their job.

Problem-centered

Surprisingly, the third approach to learning and development is often neglected in performance development. It's more commonly referred to as problem-based learning. Problem-based learning is basically about dealing confidently and competently with unexpected or unusual problems and dilemmas that people face in their job. As we discussed in Part I, with the world of work and life becoming increasingly complex and unpredictable, people must learn to think on their feet more so. There's often no process or procedure to follow in multifarious situations and people must figure out what to do—and do it quickly.

I vividly recall a recent speaking trip to Taiwan. Having eaten one of the best Thai meals ever, I approached the receptionist with gusto in the five-star motel where I was staying. As I approached the receptionist, she was beaming. "Good evening, Dr Baker. Did you enjoy your dinner?" "I certainly did!" "May I ask a request please?" "Certainly. How can I help?" came the receptionist's enthusiastic reply. "I just had the most wonderful meal in the Thai restaurant. Do you think I could get a copy of the recipe please to take home with me?" I asked, clutching a copy of the menu in my hand. There was a long awkward pause. The smile evaporated from the receptionist's face. Mild panic set in. The blood drained out of her face. I could see she was struggling. She wanted to look under the receptionist desk for the 'procedures manual' to tell her what to say and do in this predicament. Of course, there'd be nothing in the manual about this request! Anyway, to shorten this story, I did get my recipe after several meetings with sundry supervisors.

My point is this: The receptionist was trained to respond to predictable requests—not to problem-solve. A suitable process on this occasion is unlikely to be written in the hotel procedural manual. Most employees in hospitality—and everywhere else—have been trained to follow specific procedures and processes, as we discussed in Chap. 1.

But as customers become more and more demanding and their demands increasingly out-of-the-ordinary, employees are often put in unfamiliar territory such as this. For that reason, learning to solve unforeseen problems and dilemmas in the workplace is crucial to success and has a big bearing on a person's ability to do their job.

Multidimensional Approach to Learning

I'd recommend adopting a multidimensional approach to learning and development within your sphere of influence. A multidimensional perspective means using all three dimensions of learning and development. In practice, a balanced approach means that approximately a third of the learning and development budget should be devoted to technical learning, a third to personal development, and a third to problem-based learning. A multidimensional approach guarantees that a team member's development is well-rounded and more helpful.

> **Where the Rubber Meets the Road …**
>
> **Lagging Team Performance**
>
> Understanding the basis of each of the three dimensions of learning can lead a manager to be more informed about their choices. For example, Georgie who is facing the challenge of overturning lagging work performance in her administration team might deal with this in three different ways.
>
> Using the person-centered approach, Georgie could take a personal effectiveness perspective. She could coach individual team members on time management tools she's learnt over the years. This will hopefully help team members to manage their workload and priorities.
>
> Considering a technical-centered approach, she may ponder the lower performance from a technical perspective. Georgie may source a competency-based training program in administrative and skill development.
>
> A third option open to her is to take a problem-centered approach. Georgie may decide to organize the team to workshop some of the unique challenges they face in their administrative jobs. For instance, being internal service providers, she may facilitate a conversation on improving interpersonal cooperation between her team and other teams. By doing this, it may generate some ideas for improving performance in the team.
>
> For Georgie, any of these approaches—or a combination of them—may help to improve lagging performance.

What Questions to Ask?

Again, the questions you ask in this conversation will vary depending on the industry and the nature of the work. They should, nonetheless, cover the dimensions of technical learning, personal development, and problem-based learning, for the reasons I just discussed.

As a guide, here are some questions that cover these three areas:

For technical learning, a good introductory question is:

- *How would you rate your technical skills on a scale of 1–10 (10 being high and 1 low)?*

It may help for you to run through the technical aspects of the team member's job. For most jobs, there are usually five to eight key result areas.

Supplementary questions may include:

- *What technical areas do you think you have mastered?*
- *What technical areas of your job could be improved?*
- *Why do you say that? Can you give me an example?*

You may have explored the content of these questions in the previous two conversations. The difference here however, is that you're looking for specific learning opportunities to capitalize on their strengths and overcome their deficiencies. Accordingly, the learning and development conversation should move on to ways and means of building on the areas identified.

Aside from the technical aspects of the employee's job, you should consider their personal development.

In terms of personal development, you could ask:

- *What are some areas that you would like to develop personally to help you become even more effective and efficient in your work?*

Follow-up questions could be:

- *Why do you say that?*
- *Can you cite an example?*

For starters, consider the employee's team, career, and innovation roles. For example, you and your team member could consider such things as communication, self-awareness, and understanding other people as part of their ability to work in teams. For their career, it might be worth reflecting on some of their innate talents discussed in the strengths and talents conversation. What learning would assist the team member to exploit their strengths to further their career? In terms of innovation and continuous improvement, what learning would improve their capacity to add value to their organizational role? The development of this role means learning to analyze risk, conduct audits, and write reports, for example.

For problem-based learning, here's an opening question:

- *What problems or dilemmas have you had to deal with over the past few months that were challenging?*

You'd probably be surprised (and disappointed) if a team member couldn't think of a situation or dilemma. That would indicate one of two things: either they're not being stretched enough in their current role or they've come to the conversation unprepared. Either way, you should invite them to consider this question further.

Key follow-up questions are:

- *What happened?*
- *How did you approach the situation?*
- *What did you learn from it?*
- *How would you do things differently next time?*

If it's relevant, you could follow-up with:

- *What knowledge, skills, or capabilities would help you deal with this issue in future?*

Problem-based learning experiences are usually less structured than the other two dimensions and can be done in-house. It might involve sitting around a table in the office and collaborating and developing some guidelines for dealing with a similar dilemma in the future, for instance. Or, it may comprise a discussion on alternative courses-of-action in a crisis. Or, it may include coaching and supporting individuals who have had—or will have—a challenging work situation to confront. By asking the questions I've outlined, you're approaching learning from three angles—you are moving the conversation past technical know-how to the two other dimensions of learning.

The learning and development conversation builds upon the previous two conversations. This conversation is designed to help foster a person's strong points and abate their weak points.

In the final chapter, I consider the innovation and continuous improvement conversation.

The Top 10 Key Points …

1. Following the strengths and talents and opportunities for growth conversations, you're ready to discuss team members' learning and development opportunities.
2. Learning is essential for individual and organizational success in a precipitously transforming world.
3. Not all learning is done in a classroom. Most learning takes place casually on the job.
4. There's a fundamental difference between training and learning—training is part of learning, but learning is not just about training.
5. While training is trainer-centered, learning is learner-centered.

6. There are three dimensions to learning and development: technical-centered, person-centered, and problem-centered.
7. The technical-centered dimension is concerned with acquiring skills and competencies that have a direct application to a job-holder's current or future job.
8. Person-centered learning—more commonly referred to as personal development—is concerned with improving the person.
9. Problem-based learning is basically about dealing confidently and competently with unexpected or unusual problems and dilemmas that people face in their job.
10. A multidimensional perspective means using all three dimensions of learning and development.

Note

1. Baker, T. (2013). The end of the performance review: A new approach to employee appraisal. London: Palgrave Macmillan.

23

Conversation 10: The Innovation and Continuous Improvement Conversation

Innovation is transforming the current state and continuous improvement is improving the current state.

I recall reading an interesting story of a car manufacturing plant in the 1980s and the impact in the workplace of cultivating an improvement mindset.

The CEO invited all employees to suggest improvements in the way the production center operated. He offered to pay anyone for their suggestion as an incentive. The CEO was prepared to pay the amount of money saved or earned from the successful application of any initiative that improved efficiency or increased effectiveness.

After some initial and understandable skepticism from the troops, one plant operator cautiously approached his supervisor. "Is the boss serious about paying people for their ideas?" After some reassurance by the supervisor, the employee asked, "Why do we keep all the lights on in the production area?"

"Excuse me, what do you mean?" asked the perplexed supervisor. The employee elaborated, "Well, nearly all the processes are automated now. Robots don't need to see. Why can't we just have the security lights on and turn out the other lights? It would save the company on its power bill."

Simple, but powerful.

True to his word, the CEO paid that enterprising employee for his cost-saving suggestion the equivalent amount of money saved on the annual power bill charges.

Everyone was happy!

In a climate of accelerated change and uncertainty, organizations and individuals won't survive—let alone thrive—unless they're continually improving. Successful companies are innovative and agile, so we are repeatedly told. The right culture is pivotal for innovation and agility to flourish. To stay ahead of the pack, sort-after employees also regularly reinvent themselves and flexibly deploy their capabilities to stay ahead of the competition. A preparedness to change is a winning mindset—one that's never comfortable with the status quo—always trying to be better.

The innovation and continuous improvement conversation puts the spotlight squarely on a changing workplace.

Although there's a lot of 'noise' about the need to be agile, there are not too many dedicated conversations about agility in most workplaces I come across. Where they do occur, they're usually after-thoughts, done superficially, and with no follow through. It's not a topic covered in the performance review. Discussing ways to produce and do things faster, better, or differently is by-passed in the appraisal—there's no time to discuss fresh ideas. People are subsequently left with the impression that doing their job well is all that counts. Being innovative and continuously improving is a secondary consideration—at best—for most employees and their managers.

Questions such as: "How can you do your tasks faster/with fewer errors/with reduced costs/with higher quality/with more customer responsiveness?" aren't usually asked, let alone satisfactorily answered. Employees are taught to follow systems and processes, hit KPIs consistently, and not display too much original thought or enterprise.

Employees explicably become complacent—they aren't actively exploring better, faster, or easier ways of producing their company's products or services. Yet, they're told that agility is paramount in a fast-changing and competitive world. It's worth repeating from Part I: Employees receive a mixed message.

A Mindset of Stability and Predictability

Most organizations are still unsurprisingly locked into the twentieth-century mindset of stability and predictability. And this conservative thinking inhibits innovation and continuous improvement. Managers set up processes and procedures and expect employees to follow these to the letter. The rationalization for a system is that it's the best way of accomplishing an activity. People are then rewarded for following standard practice and criticized, or even punished, for not doing so. Under this straight-jacket mentality, it's tough to promote agility.

People are understandably confused about what to do, or not do. They're expected to follow standard operating procedures, on the one hand. On the other hand, they're supposed to be enterprising—to offer alternative ways to doing the work that needs doing. That's a hard juggling act. The default position taken when put in this jam is to take the path of least resistance. And that path is to faithfully observe orthodox work practices. It's less risky and undoubtedly the safest route.

But the warp speed of change calls for the ground-breaking route to be on the table for discussion. The dilemma for the twenty-first-century organization is that it should be both stable and enterprising. This is what Charles O'Reilly and Michael Tushman refer to as the "ambidextrous organization."[1] Survival and success depends on ambidexterity. The high performing organization—whether it's private, public, or not-for-profit—needs to unleash the enterprising talents of employees. Managers place too much reliance on the formulaic way and too little attention on generating original ideas.

An overreliance on compliance is essentially about control. Managers can measure and monitor acquiescence. An employee's performance can be easily evaluated against a set criterion, namely, a KPI. Have you noticed we live in a world more and more fixated with KPIs and QA? By assessing the employee against these indicators, the manager can simplify and standardize work tasks, activities, and projects. But the climate we operate in—with its abrupt season changes—demands inventiveness and creativity. Striking the right balance between compliance and enterprise is the challenge.

Most decisions can be categorized in three ways. Some decisions are black and white. In these situations, the apt response is to follow the plan without a moment's hesitation. Most decisions around safety spring to mind, for example.

Conversely, some decisions call for an original solution. For example, a truck driver delivering products to a customer may notice that the business is short staffed at the time of delivery. Although not conventional, instead of immediately moving off to the next delivery after unloading the merchandise, he elects to help his customer store the product in the warehouse. This is appreciated by the receiving company and generates goodwill—strengthening the possibility for future orders for the firm, despite its unconventionality.

The third type of decision is a Catch-22: *Do I follow the rules, or do I show initiative?* This category—which is neither black and white nor blue sky—is where decision-making is tested. In these gray areas, the safest route is to follow due process, even when displaying initiative—with its associated risks—could attain a superior result.

For example, Greta is in-charge of purchasing a product in a large corporation with stringent purchasing rules and regulations. One of those policies is to order the product on the last day of each month. Greta has heard from a reliable source that her company has won a large contract with a new customer. This customer requires immediate delivery of a large order. She decides to order outside the normal ordering cycle in anticipation of this new customer's needs. Greta's enterprising behavior violates a major company policy; it's nevertheless in the interests of the new customer and ultimately, her company.

Not everyone thinks—or is encouraged to think—like Greta. Most employees fail to be proactive in this kind of situation and default to towing the party line. But it's in these scenarios—where things aren't necessarily straightforward—that managers struggle to foster initiative. These complex choices should be discussed, preferably before deciding, but at the very least, after the event. Through debriefing, the leader and team member can agree upon what ought to be done in similar circumstances in the future. This builds confidence.

> **Where the Rubber Meets the Road …**
>
> **A Random Act of Kindness**
>
> *Southwest's* senior vice president for corporate communication, Ginger Hardage, told participants at a conference a story about one of their pilots several years ago:
> "On September 11, 2001, after terrorists had brought the 'Twin Towers' down, all other planes that were already in the air were grounded. A Southwest plane was directed to land at an airport that Southwest did not serve, and the passengers and crew were put up in a hotel. When Southwest management called the hotel to enquire about the passengers and crew, they were told that no one was there—the pilot had taken everyone from the plane out to the movies. There is no manual from which to learn that," said Hardage.
> "At Southwest, employees are encouraged to make decisions from the heart, and in turn, these proactive gestures provide positive benefits to the customers and the company."[2]

This Southwest pilot was comfortable expressing their initiative in a corporate culture espousing genuine commitment to servicing the needs of their customers. At the time of this incident, Southwest also cultivated a culture of innovation and continuous improvement. The pilot didn't feel hamstrung in expressing this random act of kindness in the extraordinary circumstances of the time. The grounding of aircraft after 'September 11' and the subsequent responses fall into this gray area, I refer to. This Southwest pilot—and all other pilots flying that day—could go one of two ways.

He could follow normal protocol in the event of a grounded plane, making sure that everyone was accounted for safely ensconced at the hotel. Or else, he could decide to do more. The pilot chose the enterprising option and entertained everyone with a night at the local cinema during an event of great uncertainty and panic. This option was despite the aviation industry—like most industries—favoring the stable and predictable decision-making route. Procedures-driven responses—rather than value-added initiative—is further reinforced by the technical-centered dimension of learning, we discussed in the last chapter. Technical-centered training stifles creativity and enterprise with its concentration on procedural learning.

This overused learning methodology teaches people to follow the 'tried and proven' pathway solving problems and making decisions. In other words, when 'such-and-such' happens, you're expected to respond in this way. It's a reactive way to problem-solve that's useful when faced with steady and predicable events. But it's not always practical when the situation warrants thinking outside-the-box.

The Difference Between Innovation and Continuous Improvement

Every industry prospers from innovation and continuous improvement. It makes sense then to discuss new and improved ways of working. The innovation and continuous improvement conversation is designed to do just that—explore ideas to improve the efficiency and effectiveness of the business.

Continuous improvement is about making progressive improvements in the way things are done. In a work context, continuous improvement means refining the way business is conducted. It should cover all facets of the workplace beyond enhancements in products and services.

Some key improvement questions are:

- How can this be done *quicker*?
- How can this be done more *accurately*?
- How can this be done in a *timelier* manner?
- How can this be done more *cost* effectively?
- How can this be done with greater *productivity*?

Continuous improvement is essentially about building upon what's already in place.

Innovation, on the other hand, is about coming up with an entirely new way of doing something. It calls for a different thought process. While continuous improvement is about how to build upon what we already have, innovation asks: *Is there a new and better way?* Briefly, innovation is transforming the current state and continuous improvement is improving the current state.

Here's an illustration of innovation. Several years ago, a local government authority I was consulting to was aware of the growing number of complaints it received from the public. Specifically, these complaints were about the length of time taken to get tombstone inscriptions completed in time for a funeral. The process was cumbersome. A relative of the deceased would draft the details to appear on the tombstone and send them off to the relevant council department. The department would subsequently complete a draft and send it back to the relative for approval. Once the member of the public had signed off on the wording and design, the council officers would then have the tombstone inscribed. This process took two weeks to complete. Relatives of the deceased became understandably upset and distressed at the length of time this procedure took, particularly when they wanted to complete the burial. This method was unwieldly, requiring several checks back and forward between members of the public and council staff. It became apparent that an entirely new approach was needed. An innovative solution was called for.

The challenge was to find a new way to speed up this approval process while being 100 per cent accurate with the transcription. An online solution was devised. In a newly created section of the council's website, the relative of the deceased would complete the wording they wanted on the tombstone plaque. The officer could immediately do a draft copy and send it back to the relative electronically for checking. Once the relative was happy with the draft, the officer commenced the engraving. This reduced the process from two weeks to one week. This new method is now common practice.

What Questions to Ask?

Here are eight dimensions to consider in the innovation and continuous improvement conversation:

- improving *quality*;
- reducing *time*;
- reducing *costs*;
- increasing *output*;
- increasing *safety*;
- meeting *deadlines*;
- enhancing *interpersonal cooperation*; and
- streamlining *systems and processes*.

Taking each dimension into consideration, here are some helpful questions, starting with *quality improvement*:

A starter question might be:

- *What quality improvements could you suggest for the products or services we provide?*

Follow-on questions could include:

- *How would you go about this?*
- *What support would we need for this to occur?*

About *reducing time*, you might ask:

- *What are some ways we can reduce the amount of time required for you and others to process work?*

Again, supplementary questions could be:

- *How would you go about this?*
- *What support do we need for this to happen?*

Regarding *reducing costs*, you could ask:

- *What cost savings have you identified in the workplace?*

This could be followed by:

- *How would you go about this cost reduction?*
- *What support do we need for this to occur?*

For *improvements in output* you could ask:

- *What system or process could be implemented to increase output, without increasing time on-the-job?*

Follow up with:

- *How would you go about this?*
- *What support do we need for this to happen?*

In terms of *safety*, you might ask:

- *What ideas do you have that might increase on-the-job safety and improve our current safety record?*

Follow up with:

- *How would you go about this?*
- *What support do we need for this to happen?*

For improvement in meeting *customer deadlines* you could ask:

- *How could we improve our record in meeting customer deadlines?*

Follow with:

- *How would you go about this?*
- *What support do we need for this to occur?*

In terms of *team cooperation*, you might ask:

- *What are your suggestions for improving cooperation between teams?*

Supplementary questions:

- *How would you go about this?*
- *What support do we need for this to happen?*

A conversation on improving *systems and processes* might start with the following questions:

- *What about our systems and processes? From your perspective, what could be improved or changed?*

And follow with:

- *How would you go about this?*
- *What support do we need for this to happen?*

You should tailor these questions to suit the industry and role you are in. Some of these dimensions will be more relevant than others. The idea is to tackle the dimensions that are most relevant to your situation. By inviting team members to select one of these dimensions that interests them, they're likely to reflect on it in greater depth.

Nonetheless, by adopting a full perspective—with eight dimensions of innovation and continuous improvement—it encourages people to take an all-inclusive appraisal of their work environment. It's a substantial step up from asking the lame question: *Do you have any suggestions for improving things?* The potential to generate ideas largely depends on the range and quality of the questions asked. Like the other four conversations in the framework, give people time to reflect on these dimensions before the conversation.

Assessing Ideas

Here are some guidelines for assessing the merits of an idea raised in conversation; you might find them useful. The criteria are based on three practical considerations—*time*, *complexity*, and *cost*.

Time

How long will the idea take to implement? The less time the better, of course. Ideas that take months or years to realize are going to be more challenging. Concepts that can be applied immediately are going to be more appealing because they are probably easier to implement. This is the low hanging fruit.

Complexity

By complexity, I'm referring to the potential drain on resources. How much impact will the idea have on the organization's resources? These resources include administrative, technical, and human.

- What systems and processes need changing to make the idea work (administrative)?
- Does the current technology support this idea—or do we need to modify or replace it (technical)?
- Who and how will people be affected by the change (human)?

The less complex the idea, the easier its implementation.

Cost

Cost of implementation must be factored in. A cost-benefit analysis needs to be thought-out, if not documented.

- What are the costs of applying the idea?
- What benefit are envisaged?

Cost is sometimes difficult to quantify. Also, it's sometimes hard to assess—or even anticipate—the benefits accurately. You need to nonetheless weigh up the idea in terms of whether the benefits offset the costs, or vice versa.

In summary, the time the idea takes to come to fruition, the degree of difficulty, and the impact upon the organization's resources all need to be assessed. A decision on the concept's feasibility can then be made with some scrutiny.

An idea that takes considerable time, is very complex, and costly, shouldn't necessarily be discounted, however. If the return is predicted to be momentous in terms of

- quality improvement,
- savings in overall costs and time, and
- increases in output and safety,

then it might be worthwhile, with more attention. A more thorough feasibility study or cost-benefit analysis may be warranted as the next step.

The criteria of time, complexity, and cost provide you with a simple analytical framework for evaluating change. If the upside is more appealing than the downside, then the execution of the idea can be defensible.

This brings us to the end of the chapter, Part III, and the book. While the learning and development conversation discussed in the previous chapter is about developing the person, the innovation and continuous improvement conversation in this chapter is about developing the organization. Being agile and responsive relies on regular deliberations at all levels of the organization. Being more attuned to possible change doesn't happen by accident. This conversation is designed to heighten awareness of organizational development.

I hope you've gained something valuable from *Bringing the Human Being Back to Work: The 10 Conversations Leaders Must Have*. If you are now having more people-focused conversations after reading my book, I'm happy. More notably, you'll probably be happier and more productive and so too—your team members.

I wish you well on your leadership journey.

The Top 10 Key Points …

1. In a climate of accelerated change and uncertainty, organizations and individuals won't survive—let alone thrive—unless they're continually improving.
2. Most organizations are still locked into the twentieth-century mindset of stability and predictability. And this conservative thinking inhibits innovation and continuous improvement.
3. The warp speed of change calls for the ground-breaking route to be on the table for discussion.
4. Every industry prospers from innovation and continuous improvement.
5. Innovation is transforming the current state and continuous improvement is improving the current state.
6. Some key questions for continuous improvement are as follows: How can this be done quicker? How can this be done more accurately? How can this be done in a timelier manner? How can this be done more cost effectively? How can this be done with greater productivity?
7. The eight dimensions for consideration in an innovation and continuous improvement conversation are improving quality, reducing time, reducing costs, increasing output, increasing safety, meeting deadlines, enhancing interpersonal cooperation, and streamlining systems and processes.
8. By adopting a full perspective—with eight dimensions of innovation and continuous improvement—it encourages people to take an all-inclusive appraisal of their work environment.
9. Assessing the merits of an idea can be done based on three practical considerations—time, complexity, and cost.
10. The criteria of time, complexity, and cost provides you with a simple analytical framework for evaluating change. If the upside is more appealing than the downside, then the execution of the idea can be defensible.

Notes

1. O'Reilly, C.A. & Tushman, M.L. (2004). The ambidextrous organization. *Harvard Business Review* (April).
2. Baker, T.B. (2009). *The 8 values of highly productive companies: Creating wealth from a new employment relationship.* Brisbane: Australian Academic Press.

Index[1]

A

ABC analysis, 187
Abuse of power, 24
Academics, 151
Acceptance, 26, 126–128, 130, 154
Accounts clerk, 176
Acknowledgement, 120, 124, 129
Action-based, 88
Adaptive advantage, viii, 26
Additional responsibility, 84
Agility, 5, 50, 204
Alexander, Graham, 71
Ambidextrous organization, 205
Amygdala, 109
Annual appraisal, 143
Antagonism, 118
Appraisal paperwork, 144
Appreciation, 41, 49, 51–55, 57, 58, 66, 80, 97, 107–109, 116, 120, 124, 128–130, 138
Apprentice, 65, 75
Aristotle, 98

Artificial intelligence, 26
Asking, ix, 17, 40, 44, 68, 69, 72–74, 76, 77, 82, 97, 116, 117, 120, 144, 161, 166, 176, 182, 187, 188, 200, 211
Assembly line, 5
Assessment centers, 32
Attention, 26, 44, 51, 55, 56, 98, 102, 110, 134, 138, 152, 178, 182, 186, 187, 194, 205, 212
Attitude, 35–37, 40, 41, 49, 53, 65, 99, 100, 108, 111, 115, 120, 162
Auditing, 90
Authentic communication, 36, 37, 49, 58, 64
Authority, 24, 37, 44, 84, 88, 90, 91, 93, 124, 208
Autonomy, 6, 8, 15, 16, 18, 24, 66, 74, 83, 87–88, 177
Awareness, 37, 90, 114, 164, 183, 191, 212

---

[1] Note: Page numbers followed by 'n' refer to notes

© The Author(s) 2019
T. Baker, *Bringing the Human Being Back to Work*,
https://doi.org/10.1007/978-3-319-93172-2

B

Baby boomers, 26
BBC, 98, 143
Benchmark, 163, 164, 166, 167, 169
Best judge, 92
Biases, 127
Blindsided, 89, 171
Bluntness, 127
Bonus pay, 14
Brainstorming, 79, 84
Buddhism, 26, 135
Budget cuts, 50
Build skill, 52
Builds trust, 49, 52, 58, 97, 185, 187
Bullying and harassment, 27

C

Camaraderie, 118, 121
Career path, 154
Carrot and stick, 8, 13–15, 18
CEO, 79, 102, 137, 203
Certainty, 26, 52, 75, 89, 154, 162
Changing world, 116
Charter, 88, 102–106
Check-ups, 92, 93
Clarity, 52, 57, 83, 85, 95, 99, 102, 105, 165
Clark, Alan, 152
Classroom, 4, 40
Classroom learning, 40, 194, 195, 200
Clear commitments, 136
Clear direction, 50, 52
Climate surveys, 163
Coaches, 37, 53, 65, 66, 69, 71, 74, 77, 98, 114, 178, 198
Co-creating, 136
Collaboration, 26, 34, 37, 43, 125
Command and control, 37
Common goal, vii, 115
Common understanding, 137
Common vision, 106
Communicating purpose, 17, 97, 100
Communication process, 89
Communication skills, 32
Communication style, 99
Comparative analysis, 164
Competence, 50, 126–128, 130
Competing commitments, 137
Complacency, 162, 169
Complex projects, 83, 85
Compliance, 16, 136, 205
Confidence, 35, 37, 45, 47, 52, 66, 75, 89, 90, 92, 99, 129, 193, 206
Confrontation, 45, 157
Confucianism, 26
Congruence, 126–128, 130
Consulting, 116, 208
Conversation culture, ix, 35
Conversation partner, 133, 134, 137
Conversation skills training, 35, 65
Corridor coaching, 67–69, 77
Counseling, 22
Countermanding, 89, 93
Courage, 45, 135
Course-of-action, 66, 74, 75, 78, 81
Covey, Stephen M.R., 126, 184
Creative thinking, 109
Creativity, 74, 138, 205, 207
Critical incidents, 43, 55, 117, 183, 190
Critical message, 136
Criticism, 7, 36, 39, 91, 124, 151, 165, 181
Criticize, 136, 185, 204
Customer deadlines, 210
Customer needs, 31

D

Data analysis, 147
DDI, 32, 37
DeChurch, Leslie, 125
Decision-making authority, 88
Defensiveness, 124, 188
Delegatee, 79–84, 90–94, 171

Deloitte's, 31, 37
Demanding customers, 114
Developmental opportunity, 17, 18, 52, 91, 93, 121
Difference-of-opinion, 56
Difficult conversations, 136
Digital explosion, 25
Disengaging, 118
Disrespectful behavior, 27
Distribution fairness, 51
Divide and rule, 118
Dixey, Angie, 37
Downsizing, 25
Downward spiral, 136, 139

E

Eastern philosophies, 25
Economy, 4, 26, 52
Edelman PR, 125
Education programs, 27
Effective management, 80, 84
Effectiveness, 32, 97, 139, 146, 148, 149, 154, 155, 158, 177, 195, 198, 203, 207
Efficiency, vii, 4, 5, 17, 146, 148, 149, 154, 155, 158, 203, 207
Electronic message, 22
Elton, Chester, 51
Email, viii, 21, 22, 34, 77, 93, 107, 134
Emerson, Ralph Waldo, 126
Emotional bonding, 25
Emotional connection, 99
Emotional intelligence, 39, 40, 46, 173
Empathetic listening, 129–130, 138
Empathy, 46, 56, 98, 111, 116, 129–130, 138
Employee happiness, 13
Employee mistreatment, 166
Employee performance, 54, 99, 100, 108, 111
Employee turnover, 52

Employee weaknesses, 173, 179
Employment relationship, 23, 24
Enabling, 74, 76
End-user, 17, 97
Energy levels, 116
Engagement, ix, 7, 16, 22, 33, 34, 37, 51, 52, 65, 69, 81, 110–112, 114, 118, 119, 121, 164, 172, 177–179
Engagement levels, 33, 116, 119
Engagement survey, 13, 25, 119, 165
Enterprise, vii, viii, 41, 50, 52, 96, 126, 177, 204, 205, 207
Enterprise performance, 33
Evaluation, 84
Exemplary leaders, 96
Expand knowledge, 52
Expectations, 37, 42–44, 46, 47, 57, 66, 74, 80, 83, 89, 93, 97, 107, 113–116, 118, 120, 126, 154, 185, 187, 189–191
Experienced leader, 89
Extrinsic reward, 3–8, 10, 14, 18, 19

F

Facebook, 25
Face-to-face, 22, 93, 102, 110, 164
Facilitate, 66, 75, 77, 78, 80, 99, 126, 152, 156, 158, 164, 188, 198
Facilitator, 156, 195
Factory assembly line, 8–10
Factory machine, 14
Fair treatment, 51, 184
Faithfulness, 127
Feedback, 17, 45, 89, 93, 97, 107, 109, 115, 119, 124, 147, 152, 157, 161–163, 171, 181, 184–186, 191, 193
Feedback sandwich, 136
Fine, Alan, 71
Ford Motor Company, 4
Fraser, Adam, 134

Frustration, 45, 66, 68, 124, 135, 139, 144
Fulfillment, 15
Full engagement, 114
Full-time work, 26
Future opportunities, 114
Future talent, 32

G

Gallup Corporation, 110, 119
GFC, 50
Global competition, 26
Goal-driven, 77, 78
Goffee, Rob, 98, 108, 129
Goleman, Daniel, 109
Good systems, 89
Good-will, 110
Gostick, Adrian, 51
Government agencies, 50
Grant, Tony, 65
Gratitude, 54, 137
Greene, Jane, 65
Growth mindset, 119
Growth opportunity, 119, 120, 155, 185

H

Hamel, Gary, 17
Hampshire County Council, 40
Hardage, Ginger, 206
Hawthrone studies, 13
Healthy, 33, 98, 100, 117, 123, 124, 126, 130, 135, 139, 156
Healthy relationship, 126, 156
High performance, 33
High performers, 154
High performing individuals, 26
High performing organization, 36, 205
High turnover, 27, 193
Human connection, 25, 26
Human dispirit, 80

Humanist movement, 7
Humanists, 7, 8
Humanize, viii, x, 17, 25, 26
Humanness, vii, viii, 27
Human productivity, 15
Human resources, vii, viii, 28, 40
Humiliation, 24

I

Ikea, 32
Improvements in output, 209
Incentive program, 147
Incentives, 6–10, 14, 203
Indignity, 24, 28, 29
Individualism, 26
Industrial history, 4, 24
Inefficiency, 165
Inexperienced manager, 45
Influence, ix, x, 3, 25, 33, 34, 65, 69, 91, 104, 114, 117, 118, 136, 166, 197
Innate talent, 54, 114, 120, 146, 172–174, 178, 179, 199
Innovative thinking, 26
Inspiration, 27, 29
Inspiring team members, 111
Interactional fairness, 51
Interdependencies, 6, 117
Interest, 9, 26, 33, 50, 55, 74, 98, 103, 108, 115, 116, 118, 120, 121, 128–130, 138, 158, 187, 206, 211
Interfering, 89, 91, 93
Internal communication, 98
Interpersonal cues, 32
Interview, 28, 145
Intimidation, 24
Intrinsic motivation, 7, 10, 18, 66, 69, 80, 83, 96

J

Janson, Kim, 36
Job description, vii, 6, 54, 119, 178
Job enlargement, 119, 176–179
Job enrichment, 119, 176–179
Job-holder, 6, 8–10, 14, 17, 97, 115, 117, 178, 195, 196, 201
Job redesign, 119
Job rotation, 119, 176–179
Job satisfaction, x, 6, 7, 9, 10, 56, 145–147, 152, 158, 161–169, 177
Job specification, vii, 5, 10, 13
Jones, Gareth, 98, 108, 129

K

Key performance indicators (KPIs), viii, 54, 204, 205
Knowledge worker, 8, 13, 15, 18, 52
Kouzes, James, 33, 96, 98, 156

L

Lack of progress, 92, 118
Language, 127, 136
Layoffs, 25, 50, 166
Leader's attitude, 36
Leadership, x, 31–34, 37, 52, 57, 64, 65, 80, 81, 91, 96–98, 100, 104, 108, 115, 120, 134, 138, 139, 156, 212
Leadership capabilities, 80
Leadership conversations, 134, 139
Leadership gurus, 96
Leadership perspective, 104
Leadership pipeline, 31, 37
Learner-centered, 194, 195, 200
Learning budget, 195
Learning experience, 65, 80, 81, 194, 200
Legislation, 27
Lepper, Mark, 3

Life experience, 66
Life's meaning, 26
Listening, 33, 40, 64, 65, 76, 98, 103, 120, 129–130, 134–136, 138, 139, 182, 187
Listening actively, 65
Listen non-judgmentally, 46
Local government, 208
Long-term goal, 109
Long-term strategies, 31
Losing control, 82
Loyal, 26, 50, 188
Lucas, Kristen, 23

M

McDonalds, 5
McManus, Joseph, 50
Management thinkers, 31, 34
Manager-centered, 156
Manager's mistake, 92
Managing priorities, 82
Managing time, 82
Manipulation, 54
Maslow, Abraham, 13
Master/servant mind-set, 24
Mastery, 8, 15, 16, 18, 52, 66, 83, 124
Maxwell, John, 135
Measurable, 88
Meditation, 26
Meeting deadlines, 183, 208, 213
Meetings, 36, 42–44, 51, 63, 67, 77, 89, 93, 103–105, 109, 113, 115, 123, 137, 155, 161, 168, 185, 197, 210
Mentoring, 154
Message, 22, 92, 107, 124, 127–130, 133, 136, 137, 163, 164, 173, 185, 204
Micromanaged, 24, 92
Micromanagement, 6, 24, 89
Millennials, 116
Mindfulness, 26

Responsive, 115, 153, 212
Result-orientated, 66
Retirement, 26
Review progress, 89
Riordan, Christine, 129
Robots, vii, viii, 203
Role, 5, 9, 10, 14, 18, 26, 28, 36, 39, 42, 44, 52, 57, 73, 76, 79, 81, 83, 85, 96, 98, 99, 110, 117, 125, 146–148, 153, 156, 162, 171, 175–178, 188, 189, 194, 199, 211
Role clarity, 83, 85
Roosevelt, Theodore, 108
Routine work, 92

Safeguards, 87, 187
Safety, 51, 67, 126, 128, 205, 208, 210, 212, 213
Sales activity, 147
Salespeople, 147
Scientific management, 4, 5, 7–10, 13, 33
Seeking clarification, 68, 74
Self-actualization, 13, 27
Self-confidence, 119
Self-critical, 185
Self-determination, 15
Self-directed learning, 66
Self-direction, 16, 18
Self-discovery, 73
Self-esteem, 14, 32, 80
Self-expression, 15
Self-motivation, 15
Self-reflection, 57
Self-reliant, 76
Self-respect, 27
Self-sufficiency/self-sufficient, 8, 24, 76, 78, 107

Self-worth, 24, 27, 29
Senior executives, 53, 80
Senior manager, 90
Sense of belonging, 14, 177
Service delivery, 50
Shared meaning, 136
Shared purpose, 136
Showing appreciation, 52–55, 58, 97, 116
Simpson, Joe, 174
Sinek, Simon, 17, 96
Skill development, 154, 198
SMART, 88
SME, 50
Social connections, 120
Social interaction, 118
Solution-focused, 66, 136
Southwest, 206
Span-of-control, 84
Specialization, 5–7, 10, 16, 177, 178
Spiritual identity, 26
Spiritual needs, 14
Standards, x, 6, 9, 42–44, 46, 52, 81, 108, 113, 151, 152, 165, 182, 190, 204
Storytelling, 98
Strategic direction, 96, 163, 182
Subordinate, 23, 77
Successful companies, 204
Succession planning, 148, 154
Supervisors, 39, 79, 80, 96, 111, 181, 197, 203
Supplementary message, 92
Supplementary question, 73, 167, 198, 209, 210
Supportive environment, 42, 44, 47
Survey results, 13, 31
Surveys, 13, 25, 40, 52, 58, 83, 88, 93, 110, 119, 163–165
Systems and processes, 51, 155, 204, 208, 210, 211, 213

T

Tangible actions, 75, 163, 169
Task-focused, 23, 34, 39–47, 55, 145
Task-specific, 22, 23, 125
Task-specific conversations, 22
Taylor, Frederick, 4, 5, 9, 10
Teachers, 3, 172
Teaching, 65
Team cooperation, 210
Team values, 99, 102–106
Technical development, 115, 120
Technical skills, 195, 198
Technology, 22, 25, 26, 34, 211
Time-consuming tasks, 82
Time-dated, 88
Trade unions, 24
Trainer-centered, 194, 200
Training courses, 72, 194, 195
Training plan, 154
Transaction, 129, 194
Transforming marketplace, 27
Truman, Harry, 91
Trust, ix, 21, 32–34, 37, 40, 49–52, 57, 58, 66, 80, 90, 97, 107, 118, 123–130, 138, 156, 185, 187
Trust assessment, 128
Trust barometer, 126
Trusting relationship, 34, 37, 41, 49–52, 57, 58
Turnover, ix, 27, 52, 162, 169, 193, 194
Tushman, Michael, 205
Two-way dialogue, 22, 145, 152

U

Ulrich, Dave, 8, 17
Ulrich, Wendy, 8, 17
Unreliable, 127
Update meetings, 89
Upward spiral, 136, 137, 139

V

Values, 9, 17, 23, 26, 28, 54, 58, 67, 96, 100–106, 116, 128, 137, 138, 151, 163, 169, 174, 199
Verbal commitment, 117
Virtual communities, 25
Vulnerable, 50, 127, 130

W

Warren, Aubrey, 67, 129, 133, 137, 138
Wellbeing, 14, 15, 184
White, Paul, 53, 55
Whitmore, John, 71
Winning mindset, 204
Wisdom, 4, 34, 68, 75, 76
Work incentives, 14
Working conditions, 114, 115, 118
Working relationship, 33, 34, 37, 41, 45, 46, 49, 108, 111, 123, 124, 130, 137, 148, 156, 167, 184
Work performance, 9, 10, 15, 18, 66, 154, 158, 175, 183, 191, 196, 198
Workplace community, 25, 27, 29
Workplace events, 117, 166
Work-setting, 14, 27, 67, 76, 95, 162, 165
World Vision, 95

Y

Yates, Simon, 174
Younger employees, 116
YouTube, 143

GPSR Compliance

The European Union's (EU) General Product Safety Regulation (GPSR) is a set of rules that requires consumer products to be safe and our obligations to ensure this.

If you have any concerns about our products, you can contact us on

ProductSafety@springernature.com

In case Publisher is established outside the EU, the EU authorized representative is:

Springer Nature Customer Service Center GmbH
Europaplatz 3
69115 Heidelberg, Germany

www.ingramcontent.com/pod-product-compliance
Ingram Content Group UK Ltd.
Pitfield, Milton Keynes, MK11 3LW, UK
UKHW021021050925
462611UK00012B/1353